Praise for
The Pocket Guide
to Inner Peace

"Gary Egeberg knows well the enemies of our happiness, and gives us the best book I've seen on inner peace since the 1950s. He brings the good news to bear in very practical ways on the tough problems of our hurt, fear, anger, and lack of self-acceptance. This brief guide helps us do our inner work, and very simply teaches us how to make prayer and meditation its foundation. It is a wonderful healing resource for both groups and individuals."

—Thomas Hart, Ph.D., therapist, spiritual guide, and author of *Spiritual Quest*

"A helpful, worthwhile resource for those who are healing their lives and moving forward."

—John Bradshaw, best-selling author of *Homecoming* and *Healing the Shame that Binds You*

"Step by gentle step, Gary Egeberg leads us on a path that is obviously familiar to him. At the journey's end, we find that we have not only attained our goal of inner peace; we have also come to rest in the arms of its Source. Thank you, Gary."

—Carol Luebering, author, *A Retreat with Job and Julian of Norwich* and *Called to Marriage: Journeying Together Toward God*

"Down to earth, practical, accessible, and helpful. Gary Egeberg offers a beautiful avenue to inner peace."

—Dr. Bridget Mary Meehan, author of 20 books, Producer of Godtalk.

"All spiritual journeys are about connecting with God, and Gary lays out the Path about as well as it can be done. All that remains is to follow where he leads."

—Earnie Larsen, speaker and author of *Stage II Recovery*

"Gary Egeberg offers us a 'serenity map' which wisely grasps two realities: Inner peace is ultimately a gift and yet there is much we can do to prepare ourselves for it and maintain it."

—Terry D. Cooper, Ed.D., Ph.D., Professor of Psychology at St. Louis Community College-Meramec, author, *I'm Judgmental, You're Judgmental* and *Accepting the Troll Underneath the Bridge*

"Offers both challenging participation and real hope that inner peace is God's gift for all people."

—Judy Logue, Formation Director, Catholic Theological Union, Chicago, author of *Forgiving the People You Love to Hate*

"The right book at the right time for guiding 21st-century pilgrims on the journey to soul-soothing inner peace."

—Lisa O. Engelhardt, editorial director for Abbey Press and author of ten books, including *Finding the Serenity of Acceptance; Acceptance Therapy;* and co-author of *Anger Therapy*

"Insightful, thought-provoking book. Great, practical ideas for achieving inner peace."

—Dr. Michael Obsatz, workshop leader and author of *Raising Nonviolent Children in a Violent World* and *Healing Our Anger*

"Inner peace isn't just for mystics anymore. This is a nuts-and-bolts handbook for any busy, stressed-out person who longs to feel peaceful."

—Harriet Crosby, author, *Living Between Jobs*

The Pocket Guide
to Inner Peace

The Pocket Guide
to Inner Peace

Gary Egeberg

Augsburg
MINNEAPOLIS

THE POCKET GUIDE TO INNER PEACE

Large-quantity purchases or custom editions of this book are available at a discount from the publisher. For more information, contact the sales department at Augsburg Fortress, Publishers, 1-800-328-4648, or write to: Sales Director, Augsburg Fortress, Publishers, P.O. Box 1209, Minneapolis, MN 55440-1209.

Cover and book design by Michelle L. N. Cook
Cover art from PhotoDisc, Inc.

Acknowledgments
Scripture passages, unless otherwise marked, are from the New Revised Standard Version © 1989 by the Division of Christian Education of the National Council of the Churches of Christ in the United States of America. Used by permission.

Scripture quotations marked Oxford AIV are based on the New Revised Standard Version of the Bible, Copyright 1989 by the Division of Christian Education of the National Council of the Churches of Christ in the USA. All rights reserved. Used by permission.

Library of Congress Cataloging-in-Publication Data
Egeberg, Gary.
   The pocket guide to inner peace / Gary Egeberg.
     p. cm.
   Includes bibliographical references.
   ISBN 0-8066-4163-0 (alk. paper)
   1. Peace of mind—Religious aspects—Christianity. I. Title.
   BV4908.5 .E44 2001
   248.4—dc21   2001033649

The paper used in this publication meets the minimum requirements of American National Standard for Information Sciences—Permanence of Paper for Printed Library Materials, ANSI Z329.48-1984.

Manufactured in the U.S.A.   AF 9-4163

05   04   03   02   01   1   2   3   4   5   6   7   8   9   10

DEDICATION

FOR MY MOTHER, THELMA EGEBERG, WITH deepest gratitude for all the love, faithfulness, and care you have shown to me throughout the years. I am especially grateful to you for your unfailing belief in me and for your many timely words of encouragement. I continue to admire you for all the tangible gestures of kindness and thoughtfulness that you have shown to so many people, not only to family and friends, but to strangers and people in need. You truly live the biblical injunction "Extend hospitality to strangers."

—Romans 12:13b

CONTENTS

INTRODUCTION

AMONG THE MOST ATTRACTIVE PEOPLE in the world are those who emanate a deep and abiding sense of inner peace and calm. From time to time we may find ourselves marveling at what seems to be their natural ability to remain centered and serene in the midst of situations that tend to leave many of us feeling frazzled, stressed, or upset. Their masterful interpersonal skills, nearly unflappable self-composure, and inexplicable magnetism are downright enviable. We wish that we could capture just a modicum of their seemingly innate ability to handle potentially upsetting situations and difficult people with such diplomacy and class. Secretly we may long for a similar depth of serenity, but are more skeptical than hopeful that this yearning could ever become a reality for us in either the near or distant future. So the wish to be as centered as they are, which is more attainable than many of our wishes, particularly if we are willing to learn and practice some "new" skills, or perhaps simply dust off some "old" ones, quickly fades. And we, just as quickly, revert to handling—or mishandling—life's stressful and difficult moments the way we always have. Occasionally we may surprise ourselves by responding to a difficult person or stressful situation in a calm and serene manner, yet we suspect that it is more of a fluke than a response we can consistently count on.

For far too many years I, perhaps like you, reluctantly accepted my lot among those for whom inner peace is more like an unpredictable visitor than a faithful and reliable companion. Peace comes and goes as it will and we sometimes appear to have very little influence over its comings and goings. On the other hand, those "naturally" centered and serene folk must either be "wired" differently or lead far less stressful lives. Or perhaps they have access to a mysterious private well of peace from which they can draw a bucketful of serenity during each of life's stressful moments. Or maybe they simply enjoy a better relationship with their Higher Power, with God, than we do. Or do they?

Take a moment to recall what you have been taught about peace during your life. I suspect that for most of us it won't take much more than a moment, for our peace "education" was sparse at best and nonexistent at worst. As a child I remember occasionally hearing the saying "when you're angry, count to ten," although it didn't seem to be practiced very often. But that's about the extent of my peace "training." If you are a woman, perhaps you or other women you know can recall learning that "nice girls" don't get angry and have painfully discovered that repressed anger and remaining silent in the face of mistreatment or injustice is among the greatest of all peace-robbers.

This is not to say that you and I never have any sense of inner peace or that we are totally stressed-out each waking hour; rather, it might simply mean that we are hungering for the priceless presence of peace more often in our daily lives. Or we may just want the serenity to stay with us for a while rather than be passive bystanders as accumulated stress or a tense exchange with a child, spouse, or coworker causes it to abruptly disappear, leaving us clueless as to when—or if—it will be back. Or perhaps we just want to be able consistently to call upon some skills and strategies to help us through those inevitable moments of inner and outer turmoil that are part of life. We not only want to have some say in peace's comings and goings, most of us would like to have a high degree of confidence in our ability to safeguard our inner peace or to help restore its presence after an unexcused and painful absence.

Even if we were not well schooled in the paths of peace during our childhood years, and many of us probably weren't, the inner peace that may indeed come naturally to the few is well within our reach. Initially we might have to learn or relearn a little bit about the nature of inner peace and discern both what we can and cannot do to bolster its presence or facilitate its return when it has been missing. We will devote ourselves to this learning, relearning, and discerning process throughout this book. We will also direct our energies toward employing some new—or perhaps merely neglected—skills and strategies to help us creatively cope with life's upsetting and stressful moments. One of our goals is to be able to bounce back quickly from the setbacks and discouraging moments we are bound to have along the way. As we learn, discern, and call upon some new or rusty skills, maybe one day in the not-too-distant future other people will admire us for our "naturally" calm and peaceful disposition and for how well we handle the upsets and stresses of life. If they only knew!

I wrote this book because I relish inner peace when it is present and suffer varying degrees of discomfort, ranging from slight to acute, when it is absent. Perhaps like you, I long for an abiding presence of inner peace in my life as well as a deeper sense of peace with God and others. Sadly, I sometimes sabotage inner and interpersonal peace by my words, actions, and inactions. I very much need to practice the suggestions I offer to you the reader and have discovered that peace frequently returns to me much more quickly when I do.

The format of this book is nearly identical to that of my earlier book, *The Pocket Guide to Prayer*. Each chapter contains suggestions or questions under the heading of "Pause, Ponder, or Practice." A prayer concludes and highlights the main points in each chapter, which is followed by three questions that are intended to serve as a catalyst for reflection, journaling, or discussion.

The Pocket Guide to Inner Peace is well suited for both individual and group use. Perhaps you will choose to read and discuss select chapters with a spouse, partner, or significant other. Or maybe some type of spirituality, church, or support group to which you belong might decide to work through one or more of the chapters together. We are in pursuit of peace together, and inner peace often grows stronger in each of us when we are meaningfully connected with others in growing, reciprocal relationships. This book might also serve as a conduit for connecting more deeply with someone in your life, perhaps a spouse, friend, coworker, teenage son or daughter, or a community to which you belong, and just as importantly, with yourself and the God who has "called you by name" (Isa. 43:1).

While the focus of this book is on inner peace, which includes peace with God and others, we might remind ourselves that our objective is not to bask in serenity while neglecting our God-given call as cocreators to respond to those in need both near and far. We are well aware of the massive and tragic suffering in our world, much of which is entirely needless. This suffering rightfully disturbs and upsets those of us on a spiritual or religious journey who have heartfelt empathy and compassion for the hungry, homeless, and hopeless as well as for the many millions who are miserable in countless other ways. And being disturbed by injustice and suffering can stimulate us to take responsible action.

One of the many payoffs for nurturing inner peace is that we develop our capacity to resist hopelessness and despair, not only in our personal and interpersonal lives, but also when we encounter incredibly complex social and global issues. As opposed to those times when we feel fragmented and anxious, a sense of being centered and peace-filled equips and empowers us to respond much more generously and effectively to those who are in need of our particular gifts, unique talents, and special ways of extending care. As we respond from our center to others in need, our own sense of inner peace is strengthened in return. In other words, we nourish and defend our inner peace, in part, so that we are able to respond in life-giving ways to our sisters and brothers. Doing so steers us away from the temptation to become self-preoccupied, which diminishes inner peace, and toward a balanced life of caring for both ourselves and for others, which fosters inner peace. The peace that we learn to nurture in ourselves not only helps us live a happier, more meaningful, and satisfying life, but it also spills over into the lives of others.

Throughout this relational dynamic, this constant inward and outward flow, God is there—rather, God is here! Our God is a God of peace who desires that we know a profound sense of personal peace in the depth of our being, in our soul. Our God invites us to be proactive in the peace process so that inner peace, interpersonal peace, and peace between and among all peoples might flourish. It is my hope that this book will inspire you to respond affirmatively to this divine invitation. It is my further hope that you will grow increasingly confident in your ability to make choices that will foster inner peace and peace with others, especially in the midst or aftermath of life's most stressful and upsetting moments.

CHAPTER 1

TOWARD INNER AND INTERPERSONAL PEACE

Our goal is peace—with others, with self, with God.

—Greg Anderson

IMAGINE THAT YOU ARE HIKING IN A LARGE forest. The beauty of this relatively unspoiled environment is truly breathtaking: tens of thousands of trees, dense undergrowth, rolling terrain, brilliant wildflowers, trickling streams, and a variety of trails and paths. Some of these paths have been well traveled and are easy to follow, while others are much rougher going because of their lack of use. Nearly every step along the more pristine and less traveled paths is a challenge as you try to avoid twisting your ankle on grass-hidden rocks or getting poked in the eye by low-hanging branches or scratched by camouflaged thorns.

Analogously, we have access to a wide variety of paths to inner peace and peace with others along our journey through life, life with all its breathtaking beauty and heartbreaking pain. Some paths that lead to inner and interpersonal peace are well worn and familiar to us; others are less familiar and a little more awkward—at least initially. When everything is going well in life, the paths to peace are easy to travel and we find ourselves living in effortless harmony with others. When life is not going so well, the paths to peace are much more difficult to traverse and our interactions with others are prone to becoming tense and turbulent.

Inner peace is likely to be marginal or nonexistent when we are at war within ourselves or embroiled in conflict with someone else and have few resources at hand to bring about a constructive, and peaceful, resolution. It is also fleeting when we futilely try to escape from certain aspects of our humanity, such as our anger, fear, judgmentalism, or an unresolved personal issue. Sometimes when our minds are churning out one negative thought after another about a particular person or group—or about ourselves—we may try with very little success to steer our thinking in a more positive direction. In fact, if we try too hard to make these peace-prohibiting negative thoughts go away, they may actually become more entrenched, which can result in terribly heavy feelings of guilt or shame.

Serenity also tends to elude a significant number of us when we avoid those persons—whether it be a relative, coworker, boss, or fellow church member—whom we consider to be somewhat abrasive, volatile, or to have some type of power over us. Perhaps they have hurt our feelings, become excessively angry with us or in our presence, or misused their power. Or maybe we simply and inexplicably feel somewhat troubled or intimidated by them. In either case we, perhaps unbeknownst to them—and to ourselves as well—may have unintentionally given our power away. This power, in some cases, perhaps even in most cases, may be something that they have neither sought nor claimed. When we avoid them or don't deal with the troubling thoughts and feelings they seem to elicit in us, we end up neglecting the personal power we have to reclaim our inner peace.

If you are periodically troubled by inner or outer conflict and wish that the turmoil would just go away once and for all, rest assured you are completely normal. Personally, I dislike conflict; no, I *dread* conflict and suspect I always will to some degree, although I have made some modest progress—amidst many, many setbacks—in dealing with its unbidden yet regular presence in my life. Sometimes when I am overly sensitive (which may be a euphemistic and more palatable way of saying slightly paranoid!) I can read—actually misread—lots of hidden motives into a person's actions, such as when someone seemingly disapproves of me, when, in fact, he or she is probably not even thinking about me! Perhaps many of us suffer needless anxiety because we try to read that which is essentially unreadable: other people's minds and motives.

In this chapter, we will discuss ten foundational guidelines that may be helpful to us on our journey toward inner and interpersonal peace. For certain we will encounter obstacles to peace on a regular basis throughout life, but these obstacles needn't overpower us or keep us unhappily stuck for an undo period of time. For instance, if we keep in mind the fact that peace is not a static condition but, like just about everything else in life, has ebbs and flows and a cyclical nature to it, we are less likely to be caught off guard when it is indeed ebbing or absent. We will also try to remember that something as basic as exercising our sense of humor, which some of us may periodically forget to do, can fling open the heavy doors of seriousness that have locked in uneasiness and locked out inner peace. But before exploring these basic guidelines about peace in greater detail, let's take a quick look at how the gift of inner and interpersonal peace is frequently manifested in the midst of daily life, as well as a few simple actions we can take to nurture its presence.

A Treasure beyond Measure

If we were given the choice between being a multimillionaire with little or no sense of inner peace and a person of modest means with an abiding sense of inner peace, most of us would probably choose the latter. Of course we'd like to be financially rich and rich in peace, but if we had to choose between the two, it is likely that inner peace would be considered the greater treasure.

This treasure of inner peace can be discovered and experienced in countless ways in the midst of everyday life. When our senses are alert, for example, peace treasures can take us by delightful surprise via a breathtaking sunrise or sunset, a unique cloud formation, singing birds, a child's smile, soft grass beneath our feet, the warmth of a hug, a gorgeous piece of music, and so on. Unfortunately, many of us at times, myself included, don't pay very much attention to our senses and to the world around us; we are too busy living in our heads and are often lost—sometimes quite literally lost—in our thoughts. Paradoxically, when we tune into our bodies, awaken our senses, and pay a little bit of attention to the world around us, the obsessive thinking that dominates us when we are upset or worried dissolves, or at least quiets down, and consequently, our thoughts become calmer and clearer.

Activating our senses enables us to keep life's upsets and irritations in better perspective so that we can bounce back more quickly when we have lost our serenity or composure. Our bodies have the healing capacity to give our minds a much-needed break if we would only invite and allow them to do so. For example, when we have been suffering regrets or remorse about the recent or distant past or are being held hostage by relentless worries about the future, we can allow our bodily senses to befriend us by listening to relaxing music, taking a leisurely bath, or going for a long walk.

Pause, Ponder, or Practice

Generate a list of ways in which you could activate your senses and allow your body to befriend you so that your inner peace might be strengthened or restored. It could be by sipping coffee or hot chocolate, listening to the autumn leaves or winter snow crunch beneath your feet, getting some exercise, hugging a child or grandchild, taking in the aroma of something you are cooking, watching children at play, basking in warm sunlight, and so on. Take a couple moments each week or each day to foster or reclaim the gift of inner peace that is available to you through your senses and by paying attention to the world around you. Try to remember to allow your body to befriend you when you are spending too much time thinking about things that sadden, anger, worry, or upset you.

Although it is not uncommon for a spontaneous sense of inner peace and well being to periodically flood our entire being out of the blue, we can also take some simple steps to experience serenity on a more regular and predictable basis. For example, we can reach out to others and enjoy the priceless gift of friendship and community and the peace that accompanies meaningful connection with others. We can also take some consistent time for solitude and enjoy quiet, refreshing self-communion. We can pause to revere nature, even if we live in a city and houseplants are the only contact we have, and experience a sense of being connected with all of life as a "natural" by-product. We can extend courtesy to someone, perhaps to a fellow driver, and enjoy an almost immediate payoff of serenity. And we can give our best to a long-postponed project at home or work and enjoy a sense of peaceful satisfaction as a result.

Inner peace can also be strengthened or restored by engaging in a favorite hobby, pastime, recreation, or creative endeavor. Personal and interpersonal peace can be enhanced by simply exercising, which decreases feelings of stress and fills us with a sense of well being, or by taking some time to read a novel that captures both heart and mind. And, of course, spending some time in prayer or meditation with the one who is in peace often opens us up to the "peace of God, which surpasses all understanding" (Phil. 4:7) as we share our worries, concerns, and problems with God.

Ten Guidelines Regarding Inner and Interpersonal Peace

During our journey through life, we regularly come upon both large and small obstacles to inner peace, some of which we place in our own path. But regardless of whether these obstacles stem from us, others, or life itself—such as an illness or accident—we usually have a choice regarding how we might approach them. We can be passive and childishly wish that they would go away on their own, which usually doesn't happen, or at least doesn't happen as quickly as we would like. Or we can approach them proactively and with an adult sense of personal power. When we choose the latter, peace-obstacles no longer need to overwhelm or immobilize us as we seek out and consider the wide variety of paths to serenity that we can take.

Just about every obstacle that we will come upon can be encountered more realistically and creatively by keeping in mind what helps and hinders inner peace. The following ten guidelines will serve as a map of sorts and equip us with some of the essential "hiking tools" to help us overcome or work our way through both the common and unique obstacles that are part and parcel of everyone's journey.

1. It is important to remember that peace is cyclical and dynamic rather than permanent and static. Life seems to be a rhythmic adventure. Of course, this rhythm is much easier to accept and flow with when we are on the upswing or on top of things than when we are on the downswing or at the bottom of the cycle. Though we may not like it, there is an inevitable downswing and bottom side to just about everything, which, of course, we usually end up resisting with monumental efforts rather than letting go and flowing with it, while trusting that an upswing is on the not-yet-visible horizon.

In our marriage, my wife and I have discovered that a rhythm of closeness and distance seem to follow each other in a cyclical and predictable pattern. We have learned that we needn't panic when we are feeling somewhat distant from each other, for a time of closeness and intimacy is on the horizon. Of course there are steps we can take to foster intimacy, but we can't force or rush it during a time when, for whatever reason, it seems to elude us.

When it comes to inner peace, there will be down times: periods when any and all peace-generating efforts seem to be ineffective and may only add to our sense of restlessness or unease. But we can be confident that inner peace will cycle up again, even though it might seem like it has left us forever. And, we can keep in the back of our mind that during those days when we are filled with inner peace, there will come a time in the future when we will experience the diminishment or absence of our serenity. So when these "down" times do indeed come, they don't take us completely by surprise. We needn't feel like we are doing something wrong, for we are simply experiencing the ebbing and flowing aspect of the inner and interpersonal peace cycle. Expecting ourselves to be able to capture and sustain serenity once and for all is not realistic; in fact, such an expectation may make the hours and days when peace is diminished or absent that much more difficult to handle.

2. Our goal is not to be pain-free or never to experience any stressful situations. Instead, our challenge is to own our pain, work through it in healthy ways, and to accept and creatively transform the stressful events in our lives. Theologian Douglas John Hall suggests that an element of struggle belongs to the created order. According to Hall, it is to be expected that we will encounter loneliness, limitations, temptations, and anxiety in the process of our development, of our becoming, as human beings.[1] These can be creative forces rather than something to be avoided at all costs. And, of course, when we are feeling anxious or lonely or tempted or when we are coming face-to-face with our limitations, there is an inevitable, accompanying element of dis-ease. Our sense of peace is likely to be diminished, but it doesn't have to be totally absent. In fact, during difficult or painful times, which we reluctantly admit seem to be a regular part of life, we can usually take one or more actions to help ourselves know at least a modicum of peace. We will explore a variety of these self-helping actions in the chapters to come.

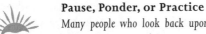

Pause, Ponder, or Practice

Many people who look back upon some of the most trying or painful times in their lives say that they grew stronger, wiser, or more whole as a result of the difficulties they experienced. In fact, they often say that if they hadn't experienced the particular pain or difficulty or loss, they wouldn't be who they are today. How have you grown as a result of some of your painful or difficult experiences? What lessons, if any, did you learn? Were you able to experience a little bit of inner peace at the time? Explain.

3. Rather than being an all-or-nothing phenomenon, inner peace ranges from a 1, or virtually nonexistent at one end of a continuum, to a 10, or deep and abiding peace at the other end. When our sense of inner peace is relatively low on this scale, such as a 1 or 2, we can take some concrete steps to increase its presence to a 3 or 4. An increased sense of inner peace rather than perfect peace is well within the realm of possibility for most of us, especially in the midst or aftermath of a stressful or conflict-laden experience. To expect ourselves to instantly go from a 1 to a 9 might not always be realistic and may set us up for unnecessary anxiety, actually delaying the return of peace. Perhaps we can think of peace increasing slowly through the intermediate stages as the tension gradually, almost imperceptibly, melts away like an ice cube.

4. Activating our whole person—intellect, emotions, body, and spirit—provides us with a wider repertoire to restore or strengthen our sense of inner peace than does our tendency to rely solely upon our minds. Obviously, clear thinking is an invaluable tool that can help us strengthen or regain our inner peace. But when encountering a particularly troublesome problem or stressful situation in life, we sometimes overthink or become obsessed, which can become another obstacle to inner peace—though we usually don't realize it at the time. Taking a "thinking break" or "intellectual time-out" of sorts in order to engage in some physical activity, listen to music, or enjoy a favorite pastime might provide us with the necessary distance so that we can return to the problem or situation refreshed in mind, body, and spirit. Too often we live most of life between our ears, either rehashing the past or rehearsing upsetting future scenarios that seldom come to pass. Remembering that we are more than our minds can actually give us peace of mind as we turn to other aspects of our humanity.

5. The passage of time is almost always required to restore inner peace, particularly after an especially intense period of upset, loss, conflict, or stress. While I wish there were an instant inner peace pill, there is none. Losing a loved one, especially in a tragic or untimely manner, may leave us feeling like inner peace has left us forever. Other highly stressful events in life such as a move, a new job, an illness, a divorce, serious family problems, faith crises, or major life-changing events are likely occasions when the passage of time will be required in order for inner peace to return to us in any significant measure. And we all know that time cannot be rushed. Nevertheless, even in the midst of very trying and difficult circumstances, we can make some healthy choices on our own behalf so that we might experience brief respites of inner peace. But perhaps it will take months, a year, or longer for the deeper and more abiding inner peace to reestablish itself in our hearts and minds.

6. Negative thoughts tend to diminish inner peace, while thoughts that are more positive in nature tend to nurture inner peace. Negativity, or what is referred to in the Twelve-Step program as stinkin' thinkin', is antithetical to inner peace. I regularly "discover" that my sense of inner peace follows my thought patterns: positive thoughts support inner peace; negative thoughts undermine inner peace. However, I am also in the process of learning that I sometimes need to welcome or at least accept my negative thoughts and allow for their expression so that they can be purged and transformed.

You may have discovered, like I have, that one negative or fearful thought often leads to another, and then to another, until the negativity or fear, like an avalanche, appears to be unstoppable. But we do have the power in most cases to stop—or at least slow down—our disturbing thoughts and gently steer our thinking in a more positive and hopeful direction. In the midst or aftermath of a bout of dark or stinkin' thinkin',' positive thoughts might not come as quickly or as powerfully as the negative ones have. And so we can easily feel discouraged and overwhelmed by our seeming inability to generate positive thoughts. But we can learn to give birth to and nurture a single positive thought, even in the midst of mushrooming negativity or accelerating fear. This fragile positive thought, when cared for as tenderly as a newborn, has the potential to grow and lead to another positive thought and then to another, having a reverse cumulative effect, so that in a relatively short period of time a measure of inner peace returns.

As you strive to replace negative thoughts with ones of a more positive nature, be extremely patient and gentle with yourself. Though there may be occasions when many of us will not be able to stop the inner negativity, especially if it has been a chronic struggle for us, there will also be times when we will have more success. Don't let a day when you can't seem to stop your negative and hurtful thoughts prevent you from trying again in the future.

7. Clinging to and reliving the past or worrying about and being excessively preoccupied with the future is an obstacle to inner peace that can be overcome by focusing on the present. I will admit that I am not very accomplished at living fully in the "present moment," but I am trying to become more so. Perhaps many of us who live in relative affluence and for whom the basics of life such as food and water are not a constant daily struggle spend far too much time reliving the past or rehearsing the future than we do living fully in the now. When I *am* able to let go of undue attachment to the past or future, peace frequently returns to me. Yet I need to relearn on a regular basis what seems to be so utterly simple: I cannot change one single aspect of the past—yet you would think I have the power to do so by how much time I spend thinking about it!—and my excessive worries about the future are usually way out of proportion to the future that actually comes to pass. The present moment is the only moment in which you and I can experience inner peace.

8. Deadly seriousness and a heavy approach to life tends to "kill" inner peace, while a lively sense of humor, especially the ability to laugh at ourselves and take life more lightly, gives new life to inner peace. Kenneth Leong says that "laughter is the beginning of liberation. . . . Self-humor is particularly helpful because it loosens up our biggest attachment—our 'self.'"[2] When you and I commit the same mistake or succumb to the same shortcoming for the one-thousandth time, we have a tendency to beat ourselves up with subsequent feelings of guilt and shame that leave us feeling even worse. A liberating and healing remedy to such peace-robbing seriousness and heaviness is to poke a little bit of light-hearted fun at ourselves. For example, instead of getting overly down on ourselves when we make a mistake or experience a moment of failure, we might say to ourselves, "I guess the world is still in no danger of me becoming perfect."

I think most of us, as well as those around us, would benefit if we were to take a much lighter approach to life. I know that I am much too serious much too often, yet when I lighten up and activate my sense of humor, I enjoy life so much more. And while the Gospels don't tell us, it is highly likely that Jesus, being such a quick-witted and keen observer of life and so comfortable in the midst of self-proclaimed saints and culturally denounced sinners, had a good sense of humor. Perhaps he was able to laugh at himself at times as well as at the nonsensical and absurd elements of his culture. Maybe humor and a lighter approach to life are elements of discipleship that have been sorely neglected, much to the detriment of not only ourselves but to all of creation.

 ### Pause, Ponder, or Practice

How readily do you laugh at yourself or at the absurd aspects of life? Can you recall some occasions in your life when taking a lighter approach would have served you better than being so serious? What current problem, difficulty, or worry might be less troublesome if you were to take a lighter or more playful approach?

9. Perfectionism tends to poison our sense of inner peace, whereas the acceptance of our imperfect humanity can serve as a highly effective antidote. The use of the word *antidote* is not too strong, for perfectionism, for expecting more of ourselves than we can possibly deliver, can poison the peace and joy right out of life, and acceptance of ourselves *as we are* can almost always help to offset this poison. (If you have not already noticed, chapters 4 and 5 are about accepting ourselves and others, including our imperfections.)

It is important to note that there is a gift element to perfectionism which can inspire us to do something well. Our desire to do something well, however, whether it is our parenting or completing a project at work, only becomes a curse or liability if we cannot accept our best and the best of others, even though both their best and our best may not be—and usually are not—perfect.

When I am in one of my perfectionist modes, inner peace is usually nowhere to be found. How hard it can be for some of us to admit that we are flawed human beings! But peace begins to return to us when, and perhaps only when, we can make this acknowledgment.

10. Giving our power away and becoming outer-referenced results in the giving away of our inner peace; reclaiming our power and becoming inner-referenced restores inner peace to us. It is so easy to give away our power to others unintentionally and let them define us and determine our self-worth. Of course, it is human nature to want people to think well of us, but when we are overly concerned with what they may think of us to the point of needing them to think well of us so that we can think well of ourselves, we have become outer-referenced.

Obviously, we don't live on an isolated island by ourselves, but among a wide range of healthy and not-so-healthy people, so others do have an influence on us and we often value their opinions. But having an influence and an opinion—the latter, of course, is not always accurate—is different than having the power we sometimes give to them to determine our value. When we have given away our power, we can always take it back and strive to become inner-referenced again. By inner-referenced, we mean that we trust ourselves, we assess our own thoughts, attitudes, and actions by our internal compass, by the values we have chosen for ourselves, rather than by the numerous and wildly fluctuating external compasses that surround us and by the values that others choose for us. We take full responsibility for ourselves, for our thoughts, beliefs, behaviors, and direction in life.

When we become externally referenced, we are flirting with or caught up in one of the painful characteristics of codependency. We allow others to determine our value, which results in us becoming unhealthily dependent upon them rather than healthily—and peacefully—independent and interdependent. Melody Beattie writes, "We don't have to give up our personal power to anyone: strangers, friends, spouses, children, [or] authority figures. . . ."[3] We can learn to value, appreciate, and affirm ourselves, rather than rely too heavily upon others to give to us what only we can give to ourselves.

While these guidelines are not in any way exhaustive, they may be beneficial to us on our journey toward inner and interpersonal peace. Let's try to keep them in mind as we address some of the specific obstacles to serenity in the chapters to come.

In the next chapter we will relearn that the way through many of our troubles and struggles usually consists of a process, which includes making progress and suffering setbacks rather than a once and for all time solution. We will also identify several specific ways to help us make some progress regardless of where we are at in that process.

Praying the Chapter

God of peace,
how deeply you must desire peace for us,
peace within us, peace between us, and peace among us!
Yet too often the whole world, including me,
seems unwilling to travel the more challenging paths
so that it might become an abiding reality.

As I journey through life,
I yearn for this treasure beyond measure,
yet I sometimes feel powerless to
restore or strengthen its elusive presence.
Sure, it surprises me with its fleeting appearances:
a child's smile, a singing bird, a much-needed hug,
but it tends to fade—or bolt—
when an unsolicited worry, regret,
or negative thought surfaces and takes me captive.

Open my heart and mind to the gift of peace.
When I feel like it has left me forever,
help me to remember that because it is
dynamic and cyclical, like most everything else in life,
it will return!
Help me, too, to do my part to bring serenity about

rather than waiting passively for it to
fall on me from without.

Finally, I ask for the grace to laugh at myself—and at life—
especially during those way-too-many-times
when my spirit grows heavy and I take
myself and everyone and everything else
with the utmost—and unwarranted—seriousness.
For the healing power of humor can restore
inner peace, and peace with others,
when I see myself and others and life itself
through lighter eyes.
Amen

For Reflection, Journaling, or Discussion

1. On a scale of 1–10, with 1 being absolutely no inner peace and 10 being a deep and abiding sense of inner peace, how would you assess your degree of peace on most days? How about today? What contributes to the presence or absence of inner peace for you?

2. What surfaces in your mind when you imagine someone who is filled with inner peace? Envision yourself experiencing this same degree of inner peace. How do you imagine yourself? What would you be doing—or not doing—to foster this sense of inner peace?

3. Of the ten guidelines regarding inner and interpersonal peace, which ones do you resonate with the most? Explain.

CHAPTER 2

PROCESSING OUR TROUBLES
AND STRUGGLES

*I don't say embrace trouble. That's as bad as
treating it as an enemy. But I do say meet it
as a friend, for you'll see a lot of it and had
better be on speaking terms with it.*

—Oliver Wendell Holmes Jr.

IN THE MIDST OF A GATHERING OF PEOPLE,
have you ever wondered what is really going on inside of
each person? Though everyone may appear to be okay from
the outside, especially when in a public setting or at a social
gathering, we can be assured that in any given group of
people at any given time, a certain number of them—of
us—are feeling less than okay. If you were to ask one of these
people how they were, it is quite likely that you would get
the automatic and society-sanctioned "fine" or "good" or
"not bad." But the truth may be that he or she—or you or
me if we were asked the same question—is filled with worries or fears or is on the brink of tears. Or this person may
actually be feeling anxious, stressed, or overwhelmed. Or
perhaps other painful emotions such as remorse, anger,
loneliness, or discouragement are much closer to the hidden
reality beneath the "fine."

If we are struggling to regain a measure of serenity
when those around us *seem* to be "at one with life," we may

discover ourselves envying one of them as we silently lament, "I wish I could be more like (name); he/she always seems to be so peaceful and happy." What we may not know is that this person might be envying us at the same time and for the same reasons, for we both may be maintaining a socially appropriate facade. Even if we are envious of someone who is truly at peace with him- or herself, we are, in Jungian terms, projecting our positive shadow onto this person. In this case, our positive shadow is the unrecognized and underdeveloped capacity for deep and abiding inner peace that we have projected onto him or her.[1] We can clearly see—or at least we think we can see—this depth of serenity in certain individuals, but we may fail to recognize it, or its potential, in us.

Sadly, we too often compare our insides, which may be in disarray, with other people's outsides, which appear to be serene. And as the saying goes, appearances can sometimes be deceiving. Thus, such comparisons are destined to be unfair to them and to us, for we are all much more complex and multifaceted than what our outsides reveal—or conceal—especially in public or social settings. Perhaps that's one reason why we have difficulty accepting certain compliments; for instance, when someone comes up to us and exclaims, "You look great! You *always* take such good care of yourself," because the way we *appear* to this person may not correspond with what is actually going on inside of us. Perhaps due to stress at work or problems at home, we, unbeknownst to our admirer, have been neglecting ourselves spiritually, emotionally, and physically for several weeks and have been feeling far from "great."

Three Basic Choices

In our society we quickly learn to keep our personal problems to ourselves, and perhaps in the majority of public and social settings it is best that we do so—at least to a certain extent. But what are we to do with these troubling problems when we are "offstage"? How might we handle these sometimes quite painful inner struggles that we so adeptly hide from others?

It seems to me that we have three basic choices. One choice we can make is to stuff whatever is troubling or bothering us. So, for example, when feeling stressed-out and harried, we might stuff these feelings deep inside rather than deal with them directly.

Another choice we can make that frequently follows upon the heels of the first choice is to impulsively and reactively pass—or dump—our stress and distress onto someone else in an aggressive or passive-aggressive manner, and thereby gain a momentary sense of relief. But because we have neither owned nor dealt with our stress directly, it is bound to boomerang back to us fueled by painful feelings of guilt and remorse for mistreating another person who, like us, also has struggles in life. When I am feeling stressed, I might snap—and, regrettably, have snapped and likely will snap again in the future (but hopefully less often)—at my wife or children, but I don't feel any better after I do. I have only succeeded in making life more difficult for the special people in my life, and for myself, as I ruminate upon my failings as a husband and parent.

Our third choice is to take full responsibility for our stress as we discern how we might deal with it in a direct manner. When we choose the latter, our stress level tends to decrease more quickly, inner harmony begins to be restored, and we are less likely to dump the worst of our-selves or what we don't like in ourselves onto someone else, thereby circumventing guilt and remorse.

While I have excelled at the first two choices, I am get-ting better at choosing option number three and feel so much better about myself when I take responsibility for my own stress, anger, fear, or whatever it may be. And those around me, including family, friends, and strangers, are also beneficiaries when I choose door or pathway number three.

Pause, Ponder, or Practice

Can you recall, perhaps like most of us, specific times and situations when you employed the first choice and tried to stuff your painful feelings or problems? How about occasions when you relied upon the second choice and took your stress or anger out on another person? In what one or two areas of your life would you like to activate the third choice and take full—or at least more—responsibility for dealing with your struggles? How would you, and perhaps those around you, benefit as a result of practicing the third choice? Visualize the inner peace that could very well be yours as you take full responsibility for dealing with this particular area of struggle or difficulty, regardless of whether or not others (if others are involved) take full responsibility for themselves.

Sometimes we may want, but seldom get, instant or easy solutions to our most persistent troubles and com-plex struggles. We need to remember that overcoming or making some modest progress with whatever is troubling us—anger, stress, worry, or what have you—often consists of a process of ups and downs, progression and regres-sion, rather than a once and for all time solution.

Before directing our attention to three basic tools that can help us creatively work our way through life's stressful and difficult moments, let's examine what's involved in the process of strengthening or restoring our sense of inner peace.

Process 101: Progress, Setbacks, and Comebacks

A process is something that takes place over a period of time. An obvious example is the process of growing from infancy to adulthood. Reaching physical adulthood is an inevitable biological process over which we have very little control; we can't—and most likely wouldn't want to—stop growing at the age of twelve or fifteen. Growing up, however, and becoming a mature, loving, and well-integrated adult is an ongoing process and the work of a lifetime.

Dealing with our troubles and struggles, our upsetting moments and painful emotions, is a process over which we have much more influence than we did when it came to determining, say, our height. Yet most of us have learned from our repeated failures to overcome our weaknesses and conquer our character flaws that we don't have total control. We can easily relate to Paul's lament: "I do not understand my own actions. For I do not do what I want, but I do the very thing I hate" (Rom. 7:15). We may want to maintain our composure in the midst of a conflict only to lose it with the very first words that come out of our mouth. We may want to live courageously, yet rediscover time and again that fear seems to be inexorable. We may want to handle stress in better ways, but periodically lose our patience with the kids when stress gets the better of us. We may long for a sense of community and connection with others, yet are hesitant to let people get close to us because we fear that they will deem us unacceptable.

In order for the transformation of a deeply rooted personal shortcoming or troubling emotion to occur we must take action, because personal peace is not likely to simply fall into our laps—or hearts and minds—while we remain passively disengaged. However, we would be wise to remember, and this is especially true for those of us who are chronic "doers," that action is not the same as activity. Sometimes we purposely stay busy (active) in an attempt to escape or avoid dealing with whatever is bothering us. Taking action, on the other hand, is a conscious choice we make to help process the discord in our lives so that inner peace might be strengthened or restored. For instance, we could choose to get some rest or even choose to do absolutely nothing for a period of time. Although both of these choices may appear to be somewhat threatening to the chronic doers among us, they could, in fact, be ways that we could take action on behalf of our inner peace.

The process of resolving an inner or interpersonal conflict or handling an emotion that we have struggled with for many years or decades, such as anger or fear, in a healthy manner is one that frequently entails making progress and suffering setbacks. We usually feel excited and pleased with ourselves when we make some surprising progress and discouraged and disappointed when we regress or backslide.

When we do suffer a discouraging setback, it tends to feel like we are back at square one, but that is almost always not the case. The progress we have made prior to the setback is real; it is not to be discounted or negated, though our feelings of disappointment, shame, or remorse and our subsequent loss of perspective may try to convince us otherwise. One key indicator that we have made and are continuing to make progress is that the setback will not keep us down for very long, not nearly as long as it may have in the past. Progress is evident after a setback or moment of regression or failure when:

- We quickly apologize or make amends to the person(s) we may have harmed.
- We spend less time and energy beating ourselves up and forgive ourselves more quickly.
- We regain our perspective and see our setback *as* a setback and nothing more than that, and certainly not as anything that detracts from our value as a human being.
- We assess what factors were at play in our setback, such as feeling exhausted or overwhelmed, and try to recognize these warning signs in the future.
- We recall specific times and situations in the past when we had a taste of success in this particular area of struggle or difficulty.
- We are able to poke a little bit of fun at ourselves and not take our moment of regression with such deathly seriousness.
- We realize that we are neither alone nor unique in experiencing setbacks, but simply an imperfect and mistake-prone human being like everyone else.
- We extend the compassion to ourselves that we would to another person if he or she had suffered a similar setback or moment of failure.

For instance, if we have recently lost our composure (which happened to me just the other day when I was discussing religion with someone), we usually feel disappointed with or even ashamed of ourselves (Why did I let that happen? I should have recognized that our conversation was going nowhere and either agreed to disagree with this person or changed the subject!). Our inner critical voice may be champing at the bit, as mine always is, to put in his or her two cents worth.

But as is often the case, a setback or regression of some type often precedes or paves the way for even greater progress. For some unknown reason, a setback almost seems to be necessary at times in order for our next growth spurt to occur. Perhaps we have another significant lesson to learn. Or maybe we need to be reminded that whenever we react in familiar counterproductive ways, such as yelling, the silent treatment, blaming, retaliation, and the like, we are setting ourselves up to suffer inevitable feelings of remorse or shame. A setback, though often painful, is not without potential redeeming value, for it frequently paves the way for a comeback and gives us the momentum to grow more than we would have had we not suffered the setback. Go figure! Personally, I would prefer to make significant progress without having to suffer setbacks, but life doesn't usually seem to work that way.

Perhaps it's like a long jumper who, after faulting on his first jump at a track meet, has to walk back down the runway in order to make another attempt. While walking back, he considers what he might have done wrong and how he can do it differently next time. And on the very next jump, he jumps further than he ever has before. Of course our process of setbacks and comebacks doesn't usually happen as quickly or spectacularly, but it does tend to follow the same pattern.

And while there is often a two steps forward, one step backward dynamic in the process of transforming inner turmoil to inner peace, we can be hopeful that as we take repeated leaps of faith, progress and freedom will indeed be possible for us, no matter what we are struggling with.

Louis Savary and Patricia Berne state that "something you experience 'in process' means you won't always be stuck with it as you are now. You will work though the problem; you will overcome the weakness; you will develop the necessary skills."[2] Being patient with ourselves over the long haul as we try, fail, learn from our mistakes and setbacks, and try again and again and again helps us develop these "necessary skills."

Pause, Ponder, or Practice

What are some aspects of your life in which you have experienced the process of progress, setbacks, and comebacks? Have you found that setbacks can be learning opportunities that prepare the way for even greater progress to occur? Explain. Of the eight signs that indicate we are making progress (see page 40), which ones are evident in your process with a particularly challenging area of struggle or difficulty?

Three Tools to Help Us Process Our Troubles and Struggles

No matter what pecks away at or robs us of our inner or interpersonal peace, and regardless of what we are struggling with or troubled by, whether it is conflict, anger, fear, worry, stress, or something else, we are neither powerless nor without choices. We can process whatever peace obstacles we encounter along the way and regain a measure of serenity by activating the less well known "three Rs" of rituals, writing, and reaching out.

1. Rituals. Rituals, ceremonies, and rites are becoming a thing of the past for many of us who live in the rational and technological societies of the West and, perhaps, of the East as well. Yet rituals, and the physicality that is a part of them, can bring new life—as well as peace—to us in a way that neither rationality nor technology can, if we exercise our creativity and playfulness.

Rituals and ceremonies have helped me to accept my painful emotions more completely, especially during those moments when I am most likely to reject them—and myself for having them. For instance, after I have expressed my anger poorly, like I did in the religion argument that I mentioned earlier, and guilt and shame are zeroing in for an all-out assault, a ritual or ceremony of some sort can help to defuse their power over me. They not only help reduce the power of these emotions, rituals and ceremonies also serve to restore my perspective as I realize once again that these painful emotions aren't "bad" and that I'm not "bad" for experiencing them, even when they overpower me and I express them poorly.

Authors Kathleen Wall and Gary Ferguson have noted that "ritual can help us replace an unhealthy outlook [toward our painful emotions] with a new perspective that enables us to see ourselves and the world [our emotional world] around us [within us] in a new light."[3] Rituals can free us from relying too heavily upon "head knowledge" about our painful feelings, which is not always stable or reliable when we are emotionally upset, in part, because of the lurking inner critic who too often causes us to lose our perspective. At the same time, rituals can strengthen the more deeply rooted and unshakable "heart knowledge" that all of our emotions are okay and that we are okay, which can help us weather and bounce back from all sorts of emotional storms.

What follows are two suggested rituals or ceremonies that have helped me process some of my troubles and struggles. They don't "work" instantly or magically, but they have helped me get unstuck, so that I might continue processing whatever is troubling or upsetting me. Usually within an hour or so I feel much better than I did prior to the ritual or ceremony. As you consider the possibility of using either suggestion in your life, feel free to adapt them as you see fit. Most importantly, trust your own ability to playfully and prayerfully create your own meaning-filled rituals and ceremonies.

A Ritual Meal: Set a table with two plates, one for you and one for an emotion that you resist, reject, or are currently struggling with. (We will once again use anger in our example. You may wish to substitute anger with a different emotion, such as fear or worry, if anger is not problematic for you.) Place two name tags, your name and the name of the particular emotion, in front of each plate. Put half of your meal or snack—it might be as simple as an apple—on your plate and the other half or portion on Anger's plate. Then sit down and share a meal with this emotion. You might even choose to light a candle in honor of your special guest. Sit in your chair for a while and eat and honestly talk to your anger, and then spend some time sitting in Anger's chair and eat and allow it to talk to you through you.

To enhance the spiritual significance of a ritual meal with this painful emotion, you might choose to break and share a piece of bread with your guest, as Christians do when partaking in Holy Communion. You might even choose to eat in silence. Perhaps you will grow in compassion for yourself and be able to acknowledge and own your anger as a result of simply sitting in Anger's chair and being fully present to it.

Of course we know that Jesus frequently ate with the rejected ones of his society, which was his way of saying "I fully accept and value you." When we eat with an emotion that we have historically rejected or denounced as being "bad," we begin or continue the process of accepting, valuing, and integrating it more fully.

Pause, Ponder, or Practice

If you were to host a meal with one of your painful or unpleasant emotions, which one would you invite? Why? (Keep in mind that the one you are most in need of sharing a meal with may be the one you least want to invite or don't like to see in yourself or others.) Consider setting a lunch or snack date with this emotion.

A Ritual of Burning or Burying: Burning is a ritual that appears often in the Bible. Burnt offerings were used by the Israelites for several reasons, including thanksgiving and contrition. We can think of offering all of ourselves, including our troubles and struggles, to God in the slip of paper we burn—or bury.

In this ritual we would take a piece of paper and write down whatever is bothering or upsetting us, whether it is a particular fear, our anger toward someone, mounting stress, our incessant inner critical voice, or a frustrating weakness. We then take the paper and burn it over some type of plate or rip it up and bury it, perhaps in a garden or compost pile, or we might simply throw it in the trash. By doing so we are taking a symbolic step toward expressing and letting go of what is bothering us. Again, there is no instant cure, but rather a significant step is taken toward releasing our pain and regaining inner peace.

One time I wrote out the anger I was feeling toward someone who had mistreated me on two pieces of notebook paper and tore the paper into manageable burning sizes. But because I then proceeded to burn the pieces of paper too rapidly, I managed to set off a smoke detector in my house, nearly scaring myself to death! Hence, I recommend burning more slowly, near water or a fire extinguisher, as well as using tweezers or pliers to hold the paper so that you don't burn your fingers.

2. Writing. It appears that the cave men and women of eons ago felt a need to write and draw some of their experiences on the walls of their caves. And child development specialists today tell us that children have an urge to write earlier than they do to read. So let's follow suit and reclaim the power and value that writing—or drawing—can have in the peace process. Keep in mind that you don't have to be a "writer" in order to benefit from writing. What follows are three suggested writing exercises that can be easily modified, expanded, or adapted, to help us process whatever is blocking the flow of inner or interpersonal peace.

Writing to Vent: Our troubling thoughts and feelings tend to circulate around and around in our hearts and minds. And like a bee that is futilely trapped between a screen and windowpane, our disturbing thoughts and painful emotions sometimes get stuck and frantically buzz around inside, leaving us with very little inner peace.

Writing can provide that tiniest of openings through which we can release and discharge our inner distress. In that sense writing can be cathartic, as it assists us in releasing the so-called unacceptable or undesirable emotions, which—especially when left unexpressed—can be such potent peace-robbers.

We can give vent to our troubles by writing in a journal or on a piece of paper that we have no intention of keeping. A good way to begin venting is to write, "I feel

_____ because . . ." or "I am struggling with _____"
or "I've had it with _____!" When we air out our troubling thoughts and feelings, especially anger, we are free to use a wide array of language—even some colorful words if we so choose—as this writing is for our benefit and not for someone else to read. If a four-letter word helps some of us release our troubles more completely and effectively than a five-letter one, then so be it. And if others of us can effectively release our upsetting feelings without the use of such words, so be it. Personally, I don't like to hear swearing, I don't advocate swearing, and I try to swear as little as possible. But when we are experiencing and trying to release an unpleasant and intense emotion, such as anger, swear words—as long as they are not directed toward someone else—may be the most effective ones for some of us to use on occasion. A saying I once heard goes like this: "There are worse words than swear words; there are words that hurt." Hurtful words that are spoken to another person are much more damaging than a "colorful" word spoken alone in order to vent one's anger.

Our goal in venting with a pen is to be totally honest. We state exactly what and how we are feeling, and the intensity of our writing should correspond to the intensity of our emotional state. Our writing, especially when we are feeling angry, doesn't have to be neat in appearance, as we certainly are not feeling very "neat" inside. We are writing for ourselves and only for ourselves, not for a former English teacher, so its legibility, spelling, and grammatical correctness are irrelevant. We can pour out our fears, discouragement, stress, struggles, or whatever is preventing us from experiencing inner peace and come to know a measure of peace as a result of our venting. It's a bit messy, much like cleaning the garage after a long winter, but we tend to feel better afterward.

Writing to Regain Perspective: When we are struggling with something that bothers us, our perspective and clarity of vision often fog over. Instead of being able to see the bigger and broader picture, we often focus—or obsess—upon what is immediately in front of us, including how upset we may feel. The wider perspective that normally guides us may become temporarily overpowered by an emotionally charged tunnel vision.

If we are feeling depressed, for example, and don't know why, writing may reveal what would otherwise remain baffling to us. Or if one day something upsetting happens at work, we may have the completely normal urge to up and quit. Taking some time to process the event via writing can give us the vision to see the situation more clearly and consider what other options are available to us besides quitting. In this case our writing may start out as venting, which decreases our emotional volatility, and as the fog of upset lifts, our thinking becomes clearer and perspective returns.

Sometimes when I have been upset and after I have poured out my feelings in my journal, I write down the words, "Perspective would say . . ." and allow the inner voice of perspective to share its wisdom with me. Perspective validates—rather than discounts—the painful emotions we are suffering. It also tends to show us more of the picture than our upset feelings may have revealed, helping us to see what our options are and how we might creatively move forward.

Writing a Dialogue or Letter: Dialoguing with our unpleasant emotions is an effective way to begin to accept them at deeper levels and process them in healthier ways. The beginning of such an interaction might go like this:

> **Me:** Hello, Anger. I really don't like you and I wish you would just go away.
> **Anger:** I have known for decades that you don't like me. But I can't leave you for I am part of your humanity. I can actually be a good friend to you if you wouldn't spend all your energy trying to get rid of me.

John Powers, in his book *Seeking Inner Peace*, dialogues with both pleasant and unpleasant emotions. He considers each of them to be a part of our rich inner world. "The complexity of our inner world is as vast as that of the outer world. Within us lives the power of fear and love, the potential for hate and compassion, as well as the motivation for building or tearing down."[4] Thus we have a need to get acquainted with and befriend our rich inner multiplicity. One way to do this is to write a dialogue in which both you and one of the feelings you struggle with speak openly and honestly to each other.

Writing a letter, on the other hand, is especially effective when we are upset with someone else. Of course, letters fall into two broad categories: ones that can be sent and ones that should *never* be sent. Sometimes writing the latter clears the emotional debris so that we can write the former in a calmer and more coherent manner. Or perhaps just writing a letter that we don't intend to send and ripping it up and throwing it away will help us process our upsetting thoughts and feelings and prepare the way for the return of inner peace. After writing such a letter, and depending upon our relationship—or lack of it—with the other person as well as the significance of the issue involved, we may discern that it is best to let it go because it is not worth further investment of our time and energy.

3. Reaching Out. The ritual and writing suggestions that we just explored can be done alone, although in some cases it might be even more healing for us to share how we are processing our troubles with a friend. For instance, let's say that you are going to write an angry letter to your boss or to your spouse that you don't intend to deliver. It might be helpful for you to share the contents of this letter with a friend before ripping it up. You are likely to feel heard by your friend and benefit from having your experiences and feelings validated. And it wouldn't be too surprising that if in the midst of sharing and talking about the letter and your boss or spouse, a burst of laughter spontaneously erupts and works its healing magic.

We might choose to reach out to a friend, but we also have the option of reaching out to our communities and to professional helpers such as pastors, priests, rabbis, and counselors, as well as to the one who is both friend and counselor—God.

Reaching Out to Friends and Community: If you or I were on a ledge and about to fall off, we would instinctively reach out for someone. Yet when we are "falling" inside we are sometimes reluctant to reach out to others, perhaps because we feel somewhat embarrassed or vulnerable or because we buy into the mistaken belief that we must deal with our problems by ourselves. And though our reluctance or hesitancy to reach out does not result in the pain of broken bones, our hurting heart and mind, especially when we go it alone, is oftentimes just as painful, if not more so.

Most of us might agree that having a caring friend show his or her concern for us in a time of need is among the most reliable remedies that will help restore our inner peace. Oftentimes these special people in our lives can provide us with incredibly wise and helpful insights regarding our predicament, as they know us and have the necessary distance and perspective to see our situation more clearly than we do when we're upset. And if we belong to some type of church group or spirituality support group, we can choose to share our troubles with members of our community, who may, in turn, feel more comfortable reaching out to us when they are troubled.

Reaching Out to Professionals: Most of us will experience at least one time, and perhaps several times, in our lives when the skills of a highly trained professional such as a pastor, rabbi, or therapist will be needed to help us work through our problems. There are a number of signs that point to our need for professional care including these three:

- The duration of what is troubling us is lasting longer than we have experienced in the past or is recurring without any sense of progress or resolution.
- The intensity of our pain is greater than what we have previously experienced and may actually be overwhelming us at times, perhaps interfering with our ability to function and cope with our daily responsibilities.
- What we are struggling with is of greater significance than a relatively minor moment of stress or conflict; for example, depression, a major change, the turmoil that often accompanies unemployment, or the grief that follows a loss.

I have gone to secular therapists with my problems and am very grateful to one in particular who has helped me process my struggles over a period of many sessions. And

I have also gone to pastors and spiritual directors for the support I have needed. I am not any more ashamed of reaching out to these caregivers than I would be of receiving medical care from a doctor if I had indeed fallen off that hypothetical ledge we spoke of a moment ago. I hope that you will set aside feelings of pride, shame, embarrassment, or whatever might hold you back, and reach out to professional caregivers when you have a need to do so.

Reaching Out to God: Friends and professional caregivers may not always be available, but God is—24 hours a day, 365 days a year. Our God is a God of tenderness and compassion and, like a parent or friend or counselor, doesn't want to see us hurting. No matter what your religious or spiritual beliefs may be, perhaps the line from the hymn, "What a Friend We Have in Jesus," says it as well as anything else; "O what peace we often forfeit, O what needless pain we bear, all because we do not carry everything to God in prayer."[5]

Turning to God is an important and helpful way to process our anxiety, stress, and upsetting moments. We frequently experience divine consolation, support, and strength when we rely upon the one who overflows with compassion. When we share our struggles with God in prayer, it is not unusual for ideas regarding how we might face one of our problems to arise within us. For example, in the midst of praying, the idea to reach out to a friend or support group might come to us.

As was mentioned earlier, the "three Rs," rituals, writing, and reaching out, are tools that can be applied to almost any situation, event, or emotion that we are struggling with or troubled by. In the next chapter, we will delve into four of the most common and powerful obstacles or challenges to inner peace: anger, fear, conflict, and stress.

Praying the Chapter

Passionate and compassionate God,
troubles and struggles are part of my life but too often
I either deny them or dump them onto anyone
nearby—loved ones, friends, strangers. . . .
Help me to deal responsibly with my own problems so that
I can enjoy inner peace as well as peace with others.

For a long time now, I have thought that some
of my feelings were bad and wrong to have.
I surely don't like it when I lose my temper,
and I'm very reluctant to let anyone know my fears.
Befriend me as I, in turn, try to befriend those emotions
that, to be honest, I would still prefer to banish.
Perhaps in the not-too-distant future I will invite
an outcast feeling to share a meal with me—and you.

I wonder, though, if I will ever be able to
retain a measure of inner peace in the midst of
life's most stressful and upsetting moments.
Although I want an instant "cure," I know it is
a process that requires my participation.
I also know that the process will entail
delightful progress, discouraging setbacks,
and courageous comebacks.

Awaken my creativity so that I might develop
liberating rituals and ceremonies to help me deal with
my persistent problems and tiresome weaknesses.

May I also help myself by venting with a pen on occasion
so that I might regain my perspective and clarity of vision.
Finally, grace me with the wisdom and humility to reach out
to supportive friends and caring professionals,
and to you, my ultimate source of support and care.
Amen

For Reflection, Journaling, or Discussion

1. What religious or spiritual rituals have had meaning for you during the course of your life? Does it make sense that rituals and ceremonies might also be able to help us deal with some of the obstacles to inner and interpersonal peace? Why or why not?

2. Have you ever written in a journal or notebook in order to vent or regain your perspective? If so, consider sharing your thoughts about it with others. Have you ever written an angry letter that you had no intention of sending? If so, describe your experience and whether or not it was helpful.

3. How readily or reluctantly do you reach out to others in the midst of a difficult time? Explain. Who can you plan to reach out to the next time you are troubled and need the support of a caring friend or community?

CHAPTER 3

DEALING WITH ANGER, FEAR, CONFLICT, AND STRESS

*It's not that I am afraid of [conflict].
I just don't want to be there when
it happens.*

—Woody Allen, adapted

IF WE WERE TO ATTEMPT TO NAME AND discuss all that either does or has the potential to spoil our sense of inner and interpersonal peace, we might be able to fill a hundred or more pages. But we will limit our discussion in this chapter to four formidable and commonly experienced obstacles or challenges to serenity: anger, fear, conflict, and stress.

Many of the other impediments to inner peace that won't be specifically addressed are often related in some manner to one of these four barriers. For instance, troubling urges to retaliate are linked, more often than not, to the ongoing struggle to express our anger in a direct and healthy manner. Our tendency to be judgmental of certain others, especially of those whose actions, beliefs, and values differ from our own, frequently correlates to an underlying and unacknowledged fear of them. The perennial difficulties we have forgiving those who have hurt us are tied to our tendency to avoid any kind of conflict with them. And our sense of being overwhelmed by or even a victim of life is related to the ways we deal with—or fail to deal with—the stress in our daily lives.

I suspect that most of us have probably wrestled with one or more of these four major obstacles to tranquility at several points along our journey. And perhaps the majority of us continue to struggle off and on with at least one of them to this day. Of the four, anger and fear have been especially difficult for me in the past and periodically overpower me in the here and now. At times I still revert to expressing my anger in reactionary rather than intentional ways. And intensifying fears can still ambush and immobilize me as effectively today as they did years ago, especially when I stuff them rather than bring them out into the open where I can assess their origin and evaluate their validity.

In this chapter we will explore in modest depth these powerful obstacles or challenges to inner and interpersonal peace. Then we will describe a fivefold method to help us deal with them, so that we can recover the priceless gift of inner peace more quickly.

Exploring Anger, Fear, Conflict, and Stress

We can expect that any one or combination of these obstacles will diminish or destroy our serenity for a period of time, because it is nearly impossible for most of us to experience a significant degree of anger, fear, conflict or stress and inner peace at the same time. But it is well within the realm of possibility to shorten the time of our distress and to reduce the intensity of our emotional discord. Let's begin by visiting our old nemesis, anger.

Anger. Our anger, as well as other people's anger, tends to trouble and even frighten us. Most of us would probably agree with clinical psychologist Fran Ferder who describes anger as an uncomfortable, painful, and confusing emotion. "The fact that it has such power is awesome both to those who feel it within themselves and to those who feel it from others."[1] And Kenneth Bakken, a pastor and physician who is committed to helping people experience the integration of body, mind, and spirit, says that just about everyone has difficulty with anger.[2] So if you, like me, periodically struggle with anger, we have a great deal of company.

When it comes to expressing our angry feelings to others in a direct and assertive rather than indirect and passive-aggressive manner, we often feel conflicted. A straightforward expression of our anger would involve the use of clear, forceful, and direct words in which we would tell the other person that we feel angry because of something that he or she did or said or failed to do or say. Using a statement such as, "I feel angry with you because (name the behavior)," not only informs the other person that we are feeling angry but tells this person why we are feeling angry. Having received valuable information, the other party might choose to discuss the situation with us, apologize if an apology is in order, or amend the hurtful behavior so as not to repeat it thoughtlessly in the future.

An indirect and passive-aggressive expression of our anger, on the other hand, could involve giving someone the "silent treatment" or withdrawing or distancing ourselves from him or her. We shut down our end of the relationship and indirectly try to punish our offender by withdrawing, whether our withdrawal is physical, emotional, or spiritual.

Part of the internal conflict we suffer with anger can be attributed to the misunderstanding that the direct expression of our angry feelings, which may be quite intense at times, might lead to violence—verbal or physical—and create an uncontrollable distance between us and the person we love. But psychologist and teacher David Richo reassures us that "anger and love coexist in authentic intimacy. Anger, like any true feeling, cannot affect, mar, or cancel real love. Anger is inevitable in any relationship in which people are free and in which they allow one another to get close. . . . *Anger does not lead to danger, distance, or violence*"[3] (emphasis added).

When we do not express and release our anger regularly, perhaps because we deem it wrong or sinful to even house such a troubling emotion within us or because we have decided that feeling angry is incongruous with being a spiritual or religious person, rage tends to grow in us. And rage, not anger, is linked to violent words and violent actions.

When we do not deal with our anger directly, we set ourselves up to be taken completely by surprise as a relatively small annoyance or irritation triggers and releases all of our unexpressed anger, which has accumulated into rage, and gushes out disproportionately to whatever finally sets us off. Afterwards, we may sheepishly resolve to not get angry again because we feel so ashamed of our excessive outburst, which only causes the cycle of stuffed anger–to mounting rage–to unpredictable explosion to repeat itself again.

Fear. Fear is certainly one of the most troubling emotions, as our fears can easily overwhelm us at times. And when we factor in its first cousin, worry, we really have our hands full. We may fear sickness, disability, old age, dying, death, and what comes after death. We might worry about losing our loved ones and friends, losing our jobs, losing our financial security, and losing our faith. We occasionally dread the uncontrollable threat of nuclear and biological terrorism and the possibility of another major war. We are sometimes afraid for our children, our parents, our neighborhoods, our country, and our world. And on and on it goes. Perhaps the Bible encourages us so many times to "fear not" because the divinely inspired authors knew what a formidable and crippling obstacle fear could be.

It's hard enough to feel fear in all its varying intensities, but what makes it even more difficult for many of us is our tendency to keep our fears to ourselves out of a sense of shame, embarrassment, or perceived weakness. This may be especially true for many men. If the saying "troubles shared are troubles divided" rings true, how much more so when we remember that "fears shared are fears divided!" Yet too often we bury them, deny them, and either refuse or don't know how to effectively—and courageously—deal with them.

Because our inner peace decreases in direct proportion to the increasing of our fears, much like the two ends of a seesaw, we need to deal with them assertively and proactively. When we were children and an older and heavier sibling or neighborhood kid kept our end of the seesaw suspended in frightening midair, we negotiated with, begged, or threatened to tell on him or her if we were not let down gently. We certainly didn't just sit there passively while this person threatened to keep us up there indefinitely, or worse, jump off!

When we encounter our "heavier" fears today, though we may sometimes feel as powerless as a frightened child, we have much more personal power at our disposal simply because we are adults. No matter if we are twenty-five or eighty-five, we can learn and practice fear-coping skills that we did not have access to as children. Unlike our less-than-sensitive sibling or childhood neighbor, the fears we experience today needn't hold us powerlessly hostage in midair.

Pause, Ponder, or Practice

How fear- or worry-prone are you? Who or what do you tend to fear or worry about the most? One effective way to reduce the intensity of your most pressing fears or worries is to examine them one at a time and discern both what you can and cannot do about it. Write down one of your current fears or worries. Be specific. Under the heading, "What I can do about this worry or fear," generate a list of actions, or perhaps it will just be one action, such as pray or talk to someone about it, that you could take to help reduce its intensity. Then, under the heading, "What is outside the realm of my control," write down what you cannot do. Finally, return to your "What I can do" heading and choose one step that you can take to address your worry or fear head-on.

Conflict. Let's just skip this one, shall we? But because it won't skip us, we, perhaps with a sense of reluctance or resignation, need to face it. Conflict is troubling to so many of us because a host of unpleasant emotions usually become jumbled together into an indecipherable conglomeration. We may feel afraid of how the person we are in conflict with will react if we were to approach him or her, or we may be more concerned that this person's feelings might be hurt by what we have to say. We might also be afraid of losing control of our anger or afraid of how our relationship with the other person could change for the worse if we were to speak our mind.

Because we feel angry, sometimes extremely so due to the importance of the issue involved or because our unexpressed anger has reached the boiling point, a knot may form in our stomach and our breathing may become short and shallow. Or we might find ourselves feeling vulnerable, self-righteous, indignant, confused, and even a bit scared and helpless like a young child. No wonder we would prefer to avoid conflict!

We also dread conflict because most of us are not particularly good at resolving it. At best, we just try to endure its unwelcome visits while hoping that it will go away as soon as possible. But it will continue to gnaw away at our peace of mind if we don't make efforts to deal with it in a healthy and creative manner.

Many of us were not taught any conflict resolution skills as children. So it is not too surprising that we might repeat what our parents, teachers, and other significant adults unwittingly modeled for us during our childhood years. Or perhaps we make some sporadic attempts at practicing healthier skills we have read about somewhere, only to automatically return to the older and more familiar ways when a particular conflict escalates. Or if we do make some periodic progress activating new conflict resolution skills, the people we are in conflict with oftentimes do not have these same skills and may react poorly, which only gives us even more incentive to avoid conflict in the first place.

This is beginning to sound pretty discouraging, so perhaps a word of hope is in order. If you are prone to running from or avoiding conflict, or if you regularly or occasionally lose your composure when you are at odds with another person and sometimes yell, cry, swear, use sarcasm, or react in some other counterproductive manner, you, along with me, belong to the majority. You might be saying to yourself, "That's hope?" Well, what if most people were good at it, and you and I were the only ones who were not good at it? But I don't think most people's conflict resolution skills are very well developed. So we needn't feel ashamed of ourselves if we have been prone to avoiding or mishandling our experiences with conflict, and discarding the burden of shame, inadequacy, or failure is a good place to start.

I'm sure that we would take heart if more people, or anybody for that matter, openly admitted that they were not good at dealing with conflict. So I'll start and you can join me if the shoe fits; maybe we'll start an epidemic. "I am not very good at dealing with conflict." To which I will add, "Ever so slowly I am getting a little better at it, but I still have room for lots of improvement."

Stress. According to psychotherapist Richard J. Gilmartin, stress is a major health problem. It affects our bodily health, "reduces our efficiency at work, and causes family strife, as it infects relationships with increased irritability, distractions, and general unhappiness." He goes on to say that little stresses can build up to the point where we finally "lose it."[4]

Trying to balance home, work, social, religious or spiritual, and other responsibilities and obligations can be quite stressful. Many of us have all the stress we can handle just from our daily commutes. Inching forward in relentless traffic week after week takes its toll. The pressures, responsibilities, and expectations that are placed on us once we get to work also take their toll. And the demands that are made of us once we return home at the end of a long day or week take their toll as well. Eventually something must give or change in our lives if we are to continue paying the many toll collectors.

We have a hunch that it is possible to live a better, more balanced, and less stressful life, but many of us firmly believe that we don't have the time or energy to make the necessary changes, even though perhaps just one small change could significantly reduce our stress levels. Instead of striving for attainable incremental changes, we sometimes complain as if our lives are completely out of our hands!

For example, we frequently tell ourselves that we should exercise more regularly but are too tired to get up any earlier in the morning or too exhausted at the end of the day. We occasionally acknowledge that we would like to read more but have discovered that it is so much easier to sit in front of the television with remote control in hand as the evening and weekend hours slip away from us night after night, weekend after weekend, year after year. Many of us will admit that we should eat healthier than we do, but junk food is temporarily comforting and fast food is all too convenient. And we know that we should nurture our spiritual life but may have drifted away from our spiritual or religious community. Or we may have completely lost our spiritual disciplines and practices, including the practice of prayer.

One of the main causes of stress—and perhaps of anger, fear, and conflict as well—is the sense of being isolated and disconnected from others. We may live in a big city and be surrounded by people every day yet be as isolated and alone as someone on a desert island. It seems to be increasingly difficult to develop the relationships and circle of support we need; this may be especially true for many men.

A significant number of men, if asked, would reluctantly admit that they do not have close male friends with whom they can share their innermost self. Some were raised with the perhaps unspoken expectation that they must be strong and independent at all times. Such an expectation makes it difficult to reach out to other men in times of weakness and vulnerability and from engaging each other at a deeper level than the veneer of such topics as sports, cars, politics, and the stock market. Perhaps most of us, women and men, young and old, feel more stressful when we are feeling alone and disconnected from other people.

We all know that stress is a part of life and that a certain degree of it is even healthy. Some pressure and stress at work calls forth our best and results in a sense of satisfaction and accomplishment. Some demands made upon us by our families and friends call us out of ourselves and into the joy of giving our best to the ones we love and care for most deeply. Some inner discomfort or dissatisfaction that arises when we are not eating well, exercising, or caring for ourselves spiritually can inspire us to take a healthy step or two on our own behalf. Instead of entertaining illusions that we might somehow be able to rid ourselves of the discomfort of stress once and for all, we can expect to experience a certain degree of it on a regular basis. Our frequent visitor only becomes harmful when we let it build up or when we fail to seek healthy avenues of release.

Obviously, much more could be said about each one of these four major obstacles to inner and outer peace. In fact, there are a number of excellent books that go into them in greater detail than we have here. Plus, it is likely that you have lived and experienced these obstacles firsthand and could—and I hope you will—add your own thoughts and understandings to our discussion. While keeping the insights from this chapter in mind as well as your own thoughts about and experiences with anger, fear, conflict, and stress, let's now examine a fivefold method that can help us deal with them.

Pause, Evaluate, Anchor, Choose, Enact (PEACE)

It is important for us to remember that dealing with such powerful peace-obliterating obstacles as these—as well as a host of others that have not been specifically mentioned such as sinking self-esteem or lingering guilt—is seldom a neat, containable, and controllable process. Spillage is bound to occur. Life is often messy and these obstacles are particularly messy; they are likely to get the best of us from time to time. By their very nature they are a bit wild, volatile, and uncontrollable—but not totally so. While we can't totally control them, they needn't totally control us either.

When we activate the following five-step method for dealing with them—pause, evaluate, anchor, choose, and enact, and perhaps other skills we have acquired—we discover that we have a great deal of peace-restoring power at our fingertips. These five steps can be completed in less than a minute or they may take us a couple of hours, a day, or longer to work through. The boundaries between them often overlap and sometimes we can take two or more steps almost simultaneously. When angry, for instance, we can pause, evaluate the source of our anger, and become anchored (centered) virtually at the same time.

Pause. Whether hounded by fears, overwhelmed by stress, caught up in conflict, or fuming with anger, we can choose to simply pause, take a time-out, step back from the fray, and put a temporary hold on the situation. When one of these obstacles—especially anger or fear—activates our sympathetic nervous system, "fight or flight," pausing helps us to quite literally catch our breath and slow down our heart rate as our parasympathetic nervous system restores our body's equilibrium.

When we are overcome with anger, we can pause and give ourselves some time, perhaps just a minute or two, to regroup. We take a time-out so as to reduce our chances of speaking or acting in impulsive and hurtful ways. When our hearts and minds are being held captive by a noisy throng of fears, we can pause to allow our fearful thoughts and feelings to wash over and through us rather than frantically and futilely fighting them. And when life becomes overly stressful, we can pause for a few minutes, an hour, a day, or longer, and remember that we have the personal power to make stress-reducing choices for ourselves. Pausing can be one such choice in and of itself. Here are some other simple and effective ways to pause:

- Remove yourself from a conversation or situation that has brought out, or that has the potential to bring out, the worst in you, the other person, or both.
- Employ one or more of the "three Rs" of ritual, writing, or reaching out.
- Allow and flow with, rather than prohibit and resist, your painful and troublesome emotions in all their intensity without doing harm to yourself or to another person.
- Delay any important decisions until you have regained your emotional equilibrium and composure.
- Get involved in some physical activity such as going for a walk, run, or swim, after which you can return to dealing with your anger, fear, conflict, or stress.
- Focus on your breathing, even for just a minute or two, so that your body and mind might become more calm through the power of breath.

- Take some time away from your regular routine and life's stresses, perhaps by going on a vacation or retreat—even for just a half-day.

Evaluate. No matter what obstacle is tripping us up, using our God-given intellect to think clearly is one of the best ways to reduce its power over us. We can feel deeply and think clearly and rationally at the same time. Of course when we are feeling intensely angry or when we are overwhelmed by fear, our emotions tend to temporarily dominate and short-circuit our capacity to evaluate the situation clearly.

Similar to those times when a fuse blows in our home and we are immersed in unexpected darkness, our ability to think clearly may be suddenly plunged into temporary darkness as anger or fear temporarily shuts out the light of reason. But it only takes the relatively minor light of a flashlight to find our way to the fuse box in order to restore the lights in our homes. So, too, it only takes the relatively minor light of remembering that we can reactivate and exercise our intellect, even in the midst of extreme stress or emotional distress, for the lights of clear thinking to be restored. We can still be feeling a high degree of fear or anger or whatever else it might be, but our feelings are reined in a bit as we reclaim our ability to evaluate the sources of our discord. For instance, the evaluative process might entail asking ourselves questions such as these:

- Why am I feeling so afraid or angry? What, specifically, is upsetting me?
- What is going on in my life that is causing these feelings to be so intense? Am I overly tired? Out of balance? Lonely?

- Has my thinking become black-and-white, all-or-nothing, and rigid? If so, what would I say to another person who was thinking—and suffering—in a similar manner? What are some grayer and more flexible thoughts that I might reintroduce?
- What is the conflict about? Is it really about me, or is it something that belongs to the other person?
- How important is it to me to resolve it? How important will it be in one month or one year from now?
- How much energy do I want to invest? Would it be wiser to let it go, or do I need to address it?
- Do I need to ask for help? Who might I turn to in order to process this situation or feeling so that I might benefit from their insights and perspective?

By asking ourselves questions such as these, we are relying upon our intellect, our ability to think clearly. We evaluate ourselves, our feelings, our thought patterns, the situation, and the other person involved—if someone is involved. Rather than passively allowing the narrower vision that accompanies anger, fear, conflict, or stress to blind—and bind—us, we activate our intellect to help us see the whole picture more clearly. By doing so we reclaim our personal power—and freedom—to deal with whatever is upsetting us.

Pause, Ponder, or Practice
The next time you feel angry, afraid, stressed-out, or are immersed in conflict with someone—maybe even with some aspect of yourself—notice what types of thoughts arise. In a nonjudgmental manner, determine if you are prone to black-and-white, all-or-nothing thinking. Assess how your thoughts either contribute to or decrease the power of whatever is upsetting

you. If they tend to make you more upset, try replacing these rigid, peace-prohibiting thoughts and self-talk with more flexible and moderate ones.

Anchor. Anchoring is at the center of our five-step method toward regaining our inner peace because it is a natural byproduct of the first two steps, that of pausing and evaluating, and preparatory for the last two steps, that of choosing and enacting. When we anchor, we focus on becoming rooted and centered before we explore our choices and put one or more of them into action.

The image of being on a boat might be helpful to us. As we are tossed about by the periodic storms of anger, fear, conflict, or stress, or in the wake of such storms, we simply drop anchor. We pause and drop anchor so that whatever upsetting obstacles we encounter along the way do not capsize us. If we forget to pause and drop anchor during a moment of anger or conflict and completely "lose it," causing our boat to overturn, we drop anchor after the emotionally charged storm has spent itself. By doing so we are able to right ourselves, regain our composure, pick up the pieces, and make the necessary amends. Furthermore, we can quickly get on with our lives knowing that even when we forget or fail to drop anchor and, as a result, react poorly, it is nothing more than yet another opportunity to learn from the experience, forgive ourselves, and ask for the forgiveness of others when warranted.

When we drop anchor, we are consciously choosing to return to our center within. This center is the very essence of our being. It is who we are at our deepest level of being, aside from any of our roles in life (e.g., parent, spouse, friend, grandparent). It is where our spirit lives in union with God's spirit. Some call it our heart while others refer to it as our soul. This center point is deep within us, a "place" in which we can tap into our wisdom and truth and God's wisdom and truth. It is a place for communion with ourselves and communion with the divine. It is a place of love and acceptance, of renewal and new beginnings. It is a resting place, a refuge, a safe haven. It is always available to us, and no one can prevent us from entering; all we need do is drop anchor.

We can be stressed-out after a particularly exhausting commute or when our children continue to bicker and fight despite numerous exhortations to stop, and simply drop anchor as we retreat to our quiet and restful place within. We can be filled with a thousand fears and drop anchor, where our fears lose a bit of their intensity in the refuge of our inner sanctuary. We can be troubled by an ongoing conflict at work and drop anchor, perhaps gaining new insights into the situation and the courage to take the necessary steps to resolve it. We can be angry because of a number of so-called "little" things that went wrong in the morning and drop anchor, so that we might regain our inner peace and salvage the remainder of the day.

Here are a handful of ways to drop anchor:

- Focus on your breathing. You can simply take ten or twenty breaths and count them as you pay attention to your inhalations and exhalations. If you notice yourself breathing in a shallow thoracic manner—from your chest—strive to breathe in a deeper diaphragmatic manner—in which your stomach goes out slightly as you inhale and returns to its normal position as you exhale. Breathing from our diaphragm for as little as a minute or two helps to diffuse our anger and dissolve our stress while restoring a sense of peace and calm.

- Repeatedly recite an affirmation such as Julian of Norwich's "All shall be well" or one that you might create particularly for the obstacle you are facing. You might call upon affirmations such as, "God's peace is within me," "God is here," or the Twelve-Step slogan "This too shall pass."
- Create and recite a breath prayer, which would be prayed in conjunction with your breathing. I have found that phrases of eight syllables or less work best. Examples include "God grant me serenity" (We might inhale on "God grant me" and exhale on "serenity."), "God, comfort me," or "Peace, be still."
- Call to mind an applicable spiritual insight you have read or discovered on your own and repeat it several times. An example might be the Bible verse "There is no fear in love, but perfect love casts our fear" (1 John 4:18). You might recast it, "God's love is stronger than my fears," and repeat it so that the truth of these words might take deeper root within.
- Spend five or ten minutes reading and meditating over a passage from one of the world's scriptures or from some other spiritual material of your choosing.
- Go for a walk or get involved in something you enjoy.
- Journal.

Choose. In this step we identify and examine our options, and then choose one or more of them to put into action in the final step. A counselor friend once told me that choosing is different than deciding in that the latter is relegated to the intellect, whereas choosing involves the use of our left brain intellect *and* our right brain intuitions, hunches, and so-called "gut feelings." We might make a particular choice, for instance, to back off from a conflict with someone, because of a feeling in our gut. Our intuition tells us that the other person is either not capable or not interested in resolving the conflict in a mutually respectful manner.

When we are caught up in an unpleasant and perhaps irreconcilable conflict with someone or when we are feeling stressed out, angry, or afraid, we sometimes forget that we have choices. We may feel overpowered by the situation or by the intensity of our emotions, but a simple way to reclaim and regain our personal power—and inner peace—is to name and consider some of our options.

I have found that talking to supportive people in my life and seeking out professional help when a situation or problem requires it have been instrumental to my ability to make good choices. I also have been fortunate enough to repeatedly come upon the right book at the right time to help me deal with a specific challenge or difficulty. During one particularly painful conflict with a person who had no intention of working with me to come up with a mutually satisfying resolution, I came upon a book that Henri Nouwen wrote when he was going through an extraordinarily painful and difficult time in his life.[5] This book was extremely helpful to me as I wrestled with a host of vindictive thoughts and painful feelings over the course of several weeks.

Some ways of generating and sorting out choices and options include the following:

• Apply Reinhold Niebuhr's Serenity Prayer to the difficult or upsetting situation you are facing: *God, grant me the serenity to accept the things I cannot change, the courage to change the things I can, and the wisdom to know the difference.* What, specifically, can't you change? What, specifically, can you change?

- Generate a written list of the choices you are considering. You are likely to come up with more choices—and sometimes better ones—by writing them down rather than by just trying to generate and sort them out in your head. You may even be surprised by the solutions that arise as you put pen to paper or fingers to keyboard. Try not to edit your choices at this point. Go for quantity. Include a smattering of irreverence and black humor as you consider your choices. Doing so may help you to lighten up a bit, so that you don't fail to recognize the best choice when it presents itself due to a heavy and downtrodden spirit. Regarding the particularly difficult conflict I mentioned a moment ago, I could have used some slightly jaded humor to help me through that painful time, such as: "I've got to ask God what on earth was going through the divine mind when this person was created!"

- Talk to someone you trust to help generate choices you may not have thought of or to confirm and affirm the ones you are considering.

- Spend some time in prayer and meditation. Ask for God's wisdom. Ask God to help you trust your own wisdom and God-given ability to choose well. We will often know that a particular choice is the "right" one for us because we will feel a sense of rightness and peace in the depth of our heart.

- Write or say aloud an "I choose to (name the action)" statement when you have determined which choice or choices you intend to put into action. Such a statement gives us a sense of personal power and response-ability as opposed to powerlessness and response-inability. For example, when tired and stressed, you might say or write, "I choose to snooze," or when afraid, "I choose to call a friend and talk about it."

- Visualize yourself putting the particular choice or choices into action as you deal with your anger, fear, conflict, or stress.[6] Mentally rehearse the scene as completely as you can. For instance, you might visualize yourself respectfully yet directly confronting someone about his or her behavior that has been hurtful to you.

Pause, Ponder, or Practice

Generate a list of choices that might help resolve a particular situation or painful feeling you are struggling with or that might reduce its negative effect in your life or in the lives of others. If you are currently pretty much problem- and pain-free, it can be something relatively minor and does not have to relate to anger, fear, conflict, or stress. The purpose is to practice generating choices so that during more difficult times and situations you might remember and call upon your power of choice. Include some playful and absurd choices in your list.

Enact. Put your choice or choices into action. Our previous four steps, which we may have employed in less than a minute or during the course of an hour or perhaps a day or longer, have prepared us to put our choice(s) into action. Putting our choices into action will not usually result in an instantaneous solution to whatever is triggering our feelings of anger, stress, conflict, or fear. But taking thoughtful and purposeful action will often help to significantly reduce their power over us and restore or strengthen our inner peace. And that, in and of itself, is no small accomplishment!

We are not guaranteed a happy ending as we enact our choices, especially when other people are involved, for we do not know how they will respond to our best efforts and intentions. They, too, have choices, including the choice to refuse their power of choice, to not be response-able. But more times than not, we will be agents of inner and inter-personal peace as we employ the choices our previous four steps have prepared us to take, for the majority of people we will encounter in life are hungering for peace as much as we are.

In the next chapter, we will discuss one of our most difficult choices, that of choosing to accept ourselves as we are at each moment, especially during our worst moments. We will also talk about some ways to forgive ourselves more completely for the times when we have hurt others and for the times when we have hurt ourselves.

Praying the Chapter

You know, God, I really don't care for
anger, fear, conflict, or stress.
I wish they would just go away but
it looks like they're here to stay.
Still, I thought I should let you know
I don't like them!
I don't like it when I get angry or when
other people get angry with me.
I hate to admit this, but just between you and me,
I feel incredibly afraid at times.
And conflict upsets me just thinking about it,
much less when I am in the middle of it!
As for stress, well, I have room for lots of improvement
when it comes to how I cope—or fail to cope!—with it.

Help me to put PEACE into practice.
I pray for the wisdom to **pause** and take a time-out
when I am upset or when a situation is getting out of hand.

Help me to use my God-given intellect to **evaluate**
whatever is troubling me rather than passively
allowing my feelings to run the show.
And thank you for the **anchor** you offer me,
for the inner sanctuary that I can turn to at any time
and rediscover that you are with me always,
ever eager to help quiet the storms in my life.

Lord, too often I forget to **choose** a better path for myself.
I confess that sometimes it's easier to pretend
that I don't have any choices when I am feeling stressed,
as I try—and fail—to pass myself off as a helpless child.
But you and I both know that
I am an adult and that I do indeed have choices
today that weren't available to me long ago.
Finally, give me the courage to **enact** one of
my choices, to take action as I deal with my
anger, fear, conflict, and stress head-on.
Amen

For Reflection, Journaling, or Discussion

1. Which of these four obstacles to inner and interpersonal peace—anger, fear, conflict, or stress—are most
troubling to you at this point in your life? Explain.
Generate a list of the potentially positive aspects of anger,
fear, conflict, and stress.

2. The third step of our fivefold method to help restore
inner peace—Pause, Evaluate, Anchor, Choose, Enact—is
to drop anchor and become centered. What helps you to
become anchored and centered during or after life's
upsetting moments? Be willing to share what works for
you with others.

3. The fourth step invites us to consider our choices and then to make a choice. Notice how often and in what circumstances you say or think the limiting words "I can't." Practice changing your "I can't" thoughts and statements to "I choose." Here's a fictitious example: "I can't put up with my boss' (or spouse's) sarcasm and negative outlook on life for one more day!" We reclaim our personal power and inner peace by changing this statement to: "I choose to ignore rather than respond to my boss' sarcasm and negative comments about life" or "I choose to confront my boss in a respectful yet firm manner about his or her sarcastic and negative comments."

CHAPTER 4

ACCEPTING AND FORGIVING
OURSELVES—IMPERFECTLY

Fall seven times; stand up eight.

—Japanese Proverb

MOST OF US HAVE LITTLE TROUBLE accepting our "good" qualities, strengths, and accomplishments, but many of us struggle—perhaps on a regular basis—to accept our shortcomings, weaknesses, and failures. We tend to feel pretty good about ourselves when the former are shining in and through us and pretty lousy about ourselves when the latter are diminishing our inner and outer light. We may even feel baffled as to how our "good" and positive thoughts and behaviors can change so abruptly for the worse. The so-called darker aspects of our humanity lying dormant within seem capable of springing out at any time. For instance, when you have been driving along peacefully and someone cuts you off or tailgates you, have you ever reacted impulsively, like I have, or had your serenity destroyed by vengeful or hateful thoughts? Or when a spouse, significant other, or partner says something hurtful to you, have you ever been chagrined by how quickly and thoughtlessly you can respond with something equally—if not more—hurtful? Or when a conversation digresses into gossip, have you ever, like me, felt uncomfortable by how hungry you are not only to listen, but to contribute your opinions as well?

As hard as our negative shadow is to accept, as in the examples above, it is a part of our humanity—although too often a rejected part. The rejected parts of ourselves can actually become a surprising source of new life as we begin the process of accepting and befriending what we consider to be most unacceptable and "unbefriendable." Sometimes heretofore unrecognized, undeveloped, or underdeveloped inner gifts begin to emerge as a result of owning, rather than disowning, what we have so often shunned, resisted, or denied in ourselves. In fact, as we get to know and befriend what we don't like in ourselves, the dualism—the duel between what is acceptable and unacceptable, forgivable and unforgivable—that causes us so much pain will begin to give way to a more holistic, integrated, and peace-filled way of approaching life.

As we learn to accept our character flaws and broken moments, and as we learn to forgive ourselves for the times we fail and fall short in life, we grow in our capacity to accept and forgive others. And as we learn to have compassion for, and maybe even to gently and nonjudgmentally cradle what we don't like in ourselves, we, in turn, may very well end up serving as an incarnate source of compassion for others who are struggling with self-acceptance and self-forgiveness.

In this chapter we will stress the importance of naming and owning what we don't like—perhaps even hate—and tend to reject in ourselves. We will also briefly probe our ongoing challenge to forgive ourselves. Then we will focus on seven suggestions to help us begin or continue the process of accepting and forgiving ourselves more unconditionally, even though our efforts, like us, will be fraught with imperfection. But knowing that we don't have to—and probably can't—accept and forgive ourselves as perfectly as we would like, may, oddly enough, actually free us to become more self-accepting and self-forgiving than we have been to date.

Naming and Owning What We Don't Like— or Even Hate—in Ourselves

If you were to apply for a job, what wouldn't you include on your résumé or mention at an interview? Or if you were to write a personal ad with the hope of meeting someone to share your life with or to simply make a new friend, what weaknesses and bad habits would you not include in your ad and not reveal during your initial conversations with this person? Or when you are with a group of friends or colleagues, what in your past—or present—is something you would not want them to know about you? Or what hurtful words or harmful actions of yours would you not want to see featured in depth on the evening news?

The personal traits, qualities, weaknesses, bad habits, and broken moments that you or I would, quite wisely, keep private in the aforementioned scenarios may reveal to us what we don't like or even hate in ourselves. They may also point to certain events in our past for which we have yet to forgive ourselves.

Many of us are too well aware of our shortcomings and persistent weaknesses, while others of us may be fighting hard to keep these unpleasant aspects of ourselves somewhat at bay. If we wish to continue growing, how-ever, we must embark—or continue—on the painful and difficult, but tremendously healing and peace-enhancing, journey of naming, owning, and accepting these so-called "unacceptable" parts of ourselves. In his reflection, "The Enlightenment," Anthony de Mello writes:

> When I try to change what I dislike in me
> by fighting it
> I merely push it underground.
> If I accept it,
> it will surface and evaporate.
> What I resist
> will stubbornly persist.[1]

Perhaps like me, you have spent most of your energy rejecting or resisting what you do not like in yourself. Yet, as Father de Mello says, what you and I resist will "stubbornly persist." Our first nonresistant task is to simply name what we don't like in ourselves. With pen in hand we might jot down our responses to questions such as these:

- What behaviors do I sometimes engage in that I wish I didn't, or that I wish I could stop but haven't been able to thus far?
- What thoughts or feelings do I sometimes have that I would not want others to know about?
- What traits or behaviors do other people have that really bug me? (The chances are that some of these traits or behaviors are present in you as well, but it may be less threatening to notice them in others.)
- What have I been wrestling with and trying to change in myself for a long time but have not experienced much, if any, success?

Important note: We would be wise to postpone naming what we don't like in ourselves when we are down, depressed, or upset. During such painful times we have a tendency to lose our perspective, which may result in us magnifying our weaknesses and character flaws way out of proportion. Our attempts to name what we don't like in ourselves could quite easily turn into a self-pecking and self-denigrating party, which would only cause us to hate our weaknesses and shortcomings even more than we already do.

But when we are on more level ground, neither too high nor too low, and name the undesirable and unacceptable parts of ourselves, we may still experience an acute sense of pain, but much to our surprise, it is often accompanied by a nearly simultaneous lessening of pain as well. It is uncomfortable to name those parts of ourselves that we have rejected, struggled with, or resisted for so long, yet a sense of relief is frequently present as we finally bring into the open what we have tended to "push underground." At some level of our being we have known all along the truth about these rejected parts of ourselves, but now we are removing a huge weight by openly naming what we have been reluctant to name.

Our next, and more difficult, step is to own what is on our list, perhaps one item at a time. These things that we do not like in ourselves belong to us, and denying them or projecting them onto others (our negative shadow) will not lead to integration or peace. To own something that we don't like about ourselves is not the same as liking it.

I don't like it when I feel angry, and I especially don't like it when I express my anger poorly, but in order to accept it—which will help my anger "surface and evaporate"—I need to own it. (My anger at that particular moment—not once and for all time—may begin to evaporate as I accept it, as I cease resisting the angry feelings that

I am experiencing.) Resisting my angry feelings, no matter how righteous or petty they may be (they tend to lean toward the latter), will lead to continued dis-integration, lack of wholeness, and lack of peace as they "stubbornly persist."

Obviously, when we own something, we acknowledge that it belongs to us. If what we own is valuable and important to us, we take special care to neither lose nor damage it.

We may own our car, for example, and don't just let anyone borrow it. Owning the so-called unacceptable aspects of our personality is a great deal more difficult than owning a car. Although we probably don't value these parts of ourselves at all, they need our special care if we are to integrate rather than be at war with them. And as with naming, we often experience a concurrent facet of pain and liberation as we own what many of us have resisted, buried, or projected onto others.

We can own what we have disowned and begin to accept what we have rejected by creating some type of ritual or ceremony or by journaling about our struggles with the particular emotion, difficulty, weakness, or shortcoming. We might also take ownership by talking with others, perhaps with a professional counselor, a friend, or those specific individuals who have been hurt by our failure to take ownership.

One simple yet helpful way to begin owning something we don't like about ourselves, such as anger, is to say aloud something to the effect of the following: "I own my anger and the fact that I sometimes express it poorly. I do not like feeling angry, and I really don't like it when I lose my temper, but I realize that my anger belongs to me. I am responsible for how I express it."

Pause, Ponder, or Practice

Take a few minutes to name and begin owning one or two things about yourself that you have tended to reject, resist, or disown. Pay attention to the feelings that you experience as you bring out into the open what you may have tried to keep hidden from yourself or others. Notice if the pain that accompanies naming and owning is tempered by a sense of relief as well.

A Word about Self-Forgiveness

No matter how strongly we may desire to live out our religious and spiritual values by treating other people—and ourselves—with the dignity and respect that we all deserve, we are bound to fail and fall short to some degree. While our hope is always to improve in this regard, we will never come close to doing it perfectly. Yet despite knowing this in a dispassionate intellectual sense, when we are in the midst of failing or suffering a broken moment, we often forget that imperfection is our lot in life. Though we are "works in progress" up until the day we die, we sometimes become impatient, exasperated, and deeply discouraged with ourselves. Surely there must be a limit as to how many times we can fail and fall short in any one particular area, much less in several areas, and still be an acceptable member of the human race! Yet as Jesus said to Peter, who thought that extending forgiveness to an offender seven times was being more than generous (three times was considered sufficient by the standards of Peter's faith tradition), "Not seven times, but, I tell you, seventy-seven times" (Matt. 18:22). In other words, we are to forgive ourselves as often as is necessary—daily, hourly, if need be—yet some of us, perhaps many of us, have never consciously forgiven ourselves even once. We have never said to ourselves, "I forgive myself for (name the offense or behavior)."

Suffering repeated failures without choosing to forgive ourselves makes self-acceptance in general more difficult and nearly impossible in any particular area of ongoing struggle, such as anger. There's little doubt that the problem we have forgiving ourselves is linked to the difficulty we have forgiving others (see chapter 5) and to the trouble we have experiencing God's unconditional forgiveness in the depth of our hearts (see chapter 6). Just as our claims to love God are rendered meaningless if we do not make attempts, however imperfect they may be, to love our neighbor and ourselves, neither can we forgive others if we do not accept God's forgiveness and take overt steps to forgive ourselves.

Growing in Self-Acceptance and Self-Forgiveness

While the process of becoming more accepting and forgiving of ourselves is something that most of us may need to work on, it is especially important—even urgent—for those of us who tend to be too hard on ourselves. Of course, we didn't just wake up one day as adults and pose the question, "Let's see, should I be accepting and forgiving of myself or extremely hard on myself and unforgiving?" and some of us masochistically chose the latter. No, for most of us, our tendency to lean in one direction or the other was greatly influenced during our childhood years by the adults in our lives, including our parents and teachers.

If you are struggling to accept and forgive yourself today, it is possible that when you were growing up your parents or other adults may have had exceedingly high expectations of you or you may have been given responsibilities that you were not ready for. Or they, perhaps quite unintentionally, may have been too hard on you or offered you a conditional type of love and acceptance based upon behavior and performance. Now, as an adult, you may feel pretty good about yourself when you are "behaving" and performing well, but not so good about yourself when you are in a slump and falling short of your—or perhaps their—standards.

Sometimes the rejection and hurt we experienced at the hands of our childhood peers may have contributed to our struggle to accept ourselves decades later. Many of us who were "teased" for being too heavy, or too something or other, still struggle to accept our bodies or whatever it was about ourselves that our peers deemed unacceptable.

All of us carry hurts and wounds in varying degrees from our childhood, as none of us grew up in perfect families or lived in perfect communities. But the good news is that if the significant wounds you suffered during your formative years are obstructing your paths to inner peace and happiness today as an adult, you can overcome your legacy. The suggestions that follow are meant to bolster this longed-for peace and happiness, as we grow in our capacity to be more self-accepting and self-forgiving.

Name one or two things that you don't like about yourself or that you tend to resist or flee from, and say aloud that you totally accept this feeling, struggle, weakness, or whatever it might be. Earlier we made a similar statement of ownership; now we make a statement of acceptance. You don't have to believe it; in fact, you probably won't believe it, but just say it three or four times, and say it aloud if possible. Here are two examples:

- "I totally accept that I am sometimes overcome by feelings of fear."
- "I completely accept that I am sometimes highly judgmental of others."

Douglas Bloch, in his excellent book, Listening to Your Inner Voice, suggests that we first need to practice accepting whatever it is that we would like to change in ourselves.[2] Transformation can only take place after or in conjunction with acceptance. Making a statement of acceptance is a wonderful first step—and one hundredth step—toward healing that we can take to help us become more accepting of those aspects of ourselves that we have labeled unacceptable.

Compile a list of your strengths, gifts, talents, and accomplishments and read it when you are struggling to accept or forgive yourself. When we are struggling with self-acceptance, our perspective tends to go out the window. Having lost sight of our personal gifts and accomplishments, our skewed and distorted view of ourselves fuels the inner critic's negative and hurtful voice. At such a time, reading and perhaps adding to our list of positives can help to restore our perspective and equip us with hard evidence to counter the critic's one-sided exaggerations and untruths.

Nothing is too small to go on your list. In fact, if you think that something is too small or insignificant, you can bet that it belongs on your list. Let's go with the motto "The smaller the better, although slightly bigger stuff is welcome, too." That way we will be less likely to discount our accomplishments and successes because we have not won the Nobel Peace Prize or negotiated a peace settlement in the Middle East. Whether you are career-oriented, deeply engaged in the vocation of caring for your children and home, or retired, you can name and claim much that is good about yourself. If your list of strengths and accomplishments is quite sparse, ask the people who know you what they think your gifts and strengths are, as well as how you have grown. You may be pleasantly surprised when they point out something that you have either overlooked or discounted.

You might choose to write down the good and positive things about yourself under these three headings: "Successes and Accomplishments," "Gifts and Strengths," and "How I Have Grown." As you consider what to include on your list, keep in mind that you can be struggling mightily in a particular area and suffering many setbacks yet still be growing. Don't think that you have to attain an unreasonable level of mastery or that you have to be free of struggle for something to go on your list. For example, I have grown in how I handle my anger and fear, even though both are still a periodic struggle for me. When I suffer a setback and am tempted to become ruthlessly self-critical, I find it helpful to recall some of the times when I have made progress in these areas.

Resist the temptation to compare yourself to others in a negative fashion, especially when you are immersed in emotional or psychological pain. If you are in the midst of making such comparisons—stop! It is human nature to do some comparing, and when we are in a good spot and feeling pretty good about ourselves, it can even be positive, as it may inspire us to emulate someone else. But when we are wrestling with self-acceptance, comparing ourselves to others is one of the worst things we can do. It is tantamount to scolding a child who falls off his or her bike for lacking the skills of a professional bicyclist. We wouldn't think of doing that, but when we compare ourselves to others, with us on the bottom and virtually everyone else above us and better than us, we are hurting ourselves just as heartlessly.

I am most prone to comparing myself to others in a negative fashion at the times when I am feeling lousiest about myself, oftentimes after I have failed yet again in a particular area of ongoing struggle. And when I succumb to and get stuck in the comparison trap, I feel increasingly bad about myself as my self-esteem sinks—or plunges— downward. Sometimes I feel like I don't have the power to stop the negative comparison, but I do and you do, too! At times like these, reading the list we put together in suggestion two, or activating one of the other suggestions, might help turn the tide so that we can once again recognize, reclaim, and celebrate our own gifts and giftedness while appreciating the gifts and giftedness of others.

Develop and call upon a circle of supportive friends. Self-acceptance is not something we do only by ourselves. As social creatures, we need the friendship, love, and acceptance of others. Irish poet and theologian John O'Donohue says we all need a soul friend, a person or persons with whom "you could share your innermost self, your mind and your heart" and be "understood without mask or pretension."[3]

And so an absolutely crucial piece of the self-acceptance and self-forgiveness puzzle involves connecting with and relying upon supportive friends with whom you can share your soul, including your struggles and weaknesses, and experience the gift of being unconditionally accepted *as you are.*

Create both "being/becoming affirmations" and "behavioral affirmations" and use them on a regular, periodic, or as needed basis. Affirmations are positive statements about ourselves as human beings (our being/becoming) or about our behavior (words and actions) that are usually written or spoken in the present tense. Affirmations have several positive benefits. First of all, they are positive statements, and positive statements about ourselves, more so than negative ones, are likely to facilitate further growth in self-acceptance and contribute to the birth and development of healthier behavior patterns. Obviously, most of us respond much more favorably to encouragement than we do to chastisement. Second, they are present tense-oriented, which helps us let go of something in the past that may be causing us pain; for instance, when we have acted contrary to our values in a particular situation and are feeling badly about it. The "present tenseness" of affirmations also calls us back from the thousand imaginative, speculative, and worry-filled scenarios we are inclined to have about the future. And third, reciting affirmations regularly, or every so often, helps us grow in both our belief and in our ability to practice what we are affirming, for belief and practice walk hand in hand together and strengthen each other.

We can affirm the behavioral changes we are striving for and we can affirm ourself as a person, as a human being. If we have had a tendency to deal harshly with ourselves when we are struggling, we might create and recite affirmations about our behavior, such as, "I treat myself gently during this difficult time" or "I am beginning to treat myself more gently, especially when I am hurting."

We can affirm ourselves as a person apart from our behavior which fluctuates on the positive-negative, gentleness-harshness continuum, such as "I am a gentle person" or "I am becoming more gentle each day." Again, with "being/becoming affirmations," we affirm ourselves at the level of our being-ness and becoming-ness, so gentleness would be claimed as part of who we are and of who we are becoming, regardless of the setbacks we suffer when we are not so gentle with ourselves or others.

Douglas Bloch teaches us that when we create an affirmation, our first response might be to reject the positive statement about ourselves.[4] So Bloch encourages us to counter our first response with a second response, so that the negativity or critical element of the first response does not have the last word. He suggests setting up three sections, as below, to which I have added parenthetical comments for the purpose of clarity:

Affirmation (*being/becoming or behavioral*):
I am a peaceful person.

First response (*rejects the affirmation*):
No you're not. You sometimes feel very irritable and anxious.

Second response (*counters the rejection*):
I am becoming more peaceful each day.

In the example above, my first response is negative, critical, and self-limiting, despite the element of truth in it. Bloch says that if we leave the first response unchallenged, it is likely to be what we will believe and experience, with the result of rendering our initial affirmation impotent. My second response, however, takes into account the element of truth in the first response: sometimes I do feel irritable and anxious. But I am *becoming*, and am in the process of evolving into, a more peaceful person, despite the fact that I neither feel serene nor act peacefully all the time. My first affirmation needed to be revised because of my initial response to it. My second affirmation (second response) is one that I can believe more easily and fully and, consequently, can help me continue to grow as a peaceful person.

Pause, Ponder, or Practice

Try composing a being/becoming or behavioral affirmation about yourself in an area in which you are weak or struggling. Remember to write it in the present tense. If you find yourself objecting to or pooh-poohing your affirmation, write down this first response. Then write down your second response, so that you will be able to believe, to some degree, what you are affirming. Note: Your belief might be weak or shaky, which is okay, because you are affirming something that has been troubling or challenging to you.

Dialogue or argue with the critical voice that says you are not acceptable or that you have done things that are not forgivable. We talked about dialoguing with an unpleasant or painful emotion in chapter 2, so this is a spin-off from that suggestion.

One reason why such a dialogue can be helpful is that it allows the self-rejecting and unforgiving voice to have its say. Part of the reason this voice can be so powerful is that we either tend to keep it inside or we try to silence it, which only makes it grow stronger. Another reason to engage in a dialogue with the inner critical voice is that it brings what has been painfully circulating around in the murky shadows of our heart and mind out into the open, into the light, where it can be seen with greater clarity and objectivity. And third, it provides us with an opportunity to dialogue with it, argue with it, counter it, and maybe even transform it. Here is one such dialogue:

Critical Voice (*self-rejecting and unforgiving voice*): You know you've done some bad things that are totally unacceptable and unforgivable during your life. Why, just the other day in fact, you yelled at your kids. That was terrible!

Me (*my truest and deepest self*): I did blow it the other day and I feel very sad about it.

CV: You should feel sad! You're a pretty lousy parent.

Me: But I apologized to my kids and told them I would try to do it differently next time. I also told them that I don't always handle my anger as well as I would like to, but I'll keep working on it.

CV: So you think that gets you off the hook? You know you're going to yell at them again.

Me: Maybe so, but it's happening less often and, like I said, I will keep working on it. I will continue to strive for progress in the midst of my setbacks.

CV: How long are you going to keep "working on it"? You know some better ways to express your anger now, but you still don't do what you know. You—

Me: Excuse me for interrupting, but I know that I don't do it perfectly and I'm not ever going to do it perfectly. I am a human being, not an infallible machine.

CV: Well, you should be farther along than you are now.

Me: Please don't "should" me. I am proud of the progress I have made. I know that when I have a setback, I will make even more progress. I'm not going to buy into the perfection trap anymore. I can't be a perfect parent, but I can be a better parent, even though I sometimes blow it. I accept myself as I am and I totally forgive myself for the times I have failed as a parent, including the other day. In fact, I'm going to name some of the many things that I do well as a parent.

CV: But wait! I have lots of other stuff to talk to you about.

Me: Later. I've heard what you've had to say about my "yelling episode" and taken it into consideration. No doubt, we will talk again—probably in the not-too-distant future—but now I am going to spend some time with my kids.

A dialogue such as the above honors the critical voice by allowing it full and uncensored expression. Dialoguing also helps the inner voice of love, our truest self, to have its full say as well, for this is a voice that is underdeveloped and underutilized in many of us. And love—of which our inner voice of love is a crucial component—by its very nature accepts, forgives, heals, and wants to let go of the pain of the past so that we can start fresh and live fully in the now.

Create a self-blessing ritual or ceremony to help you accept and forgive yourself. One self-blessing ritual in particular has been especially helpful to me when I have been overpowered by feelings of remorse or shame for having acted poorly. In this ritual, you would dip your finger into a bowl or cup of water and bless yourself by tracing a symbol that has meaning for you—perhaps a cross, the Star of David, a heart, the peace sign, a circle—on your temple, lips, and chest. (This ritual is adapted from the Catholic practice of tracing the sign of the cross on the forehead, lips, and heart just before the gospel is read at Mass.)

Tracing the symbol on your temple is a ritual self-blessing to help foster peace of mind and to put an end to the discordant and harsh thoughts you may be having about yourself or others. Tracing the symbol on your lips can be a symbolic gesture to nurture the peaceful words you desire to speak to and about yourself and others. Tracing it on your chest is a tangible gesture to help quiet and soothe the heartaches you are suffering from at the time.

Water literally cleanses us, and the ritual use of water in a self-blessing ceremony can symbolically cleanse us of the burdens and hurts that we are carrying. Many of us are hurting and burdened because of an inclination to reject some aspects of our body, or even our whole body. We can trace our chosen symbol on the particular part of our body we may be struggling to accept, or all over our body as a ritual gesture of acceptance of our body as it is, even though we may want it to be different than it is.

When I have done this particular self-blessing ritual, I have found it helpful to speak aloud healing words of forgiveness and acceptance to myself. "I forgive myself for yelling at my kids." "I forgive and accept myself for being judgmental of others." "I accept my body as it is." I urge you to call forth your creativity and experiment with self-blessing rituals and ceremonies that have the potential to help heal you in your most wounded places.

Pause, Ponder, or Practice

Consider developing a self-blessing ritual of some type. You might ask those who are closest to you to participate in your ritual, perhaps by adding their blessing of you to your self-blessing. You might be so empowered that you will choose to ritually bless some of the special people in your life, perhaps including your children or grandchildren.

Earlier in the chapter, we pondered a portion of Anthony de Mello's reflection, "The Enlightenment." Because it is so applicable to what we have discussed in this chapter, as well as to what we will explore in the next chapter when we address the difficult task of accepting and forgiving others, here it is in its entirety. The space after each segment is meant to encourage a meditative pause.

The Enlightenment
When I try to change what I dislike in me
by fighting it
I merely push it underground.
If I accept it,
it will surface and evaporate.
What I resist
will stubbornly persist.

I consider the example of Jesus, who sets himself the task of moving mountains and battles with exasperating foes. Yet even in his anger he is loving—he combines a keen desire for change with an acceptance of reality as it is.

I try to be like him.
I start with feelings I dislike.
To each of them I talk
in a loving, accepting kind of way
and listen to what each has to say,
till I discover that, while it can do me harm,
it also does me good,
that it is there for a benign purpose,
which I now attempt to see.

I keep on with the dialogue
till I feel a real acceptance of these feelings

—acceptance, not approval, not resignation—
so that I am no longer depressed about my depressions
or angry with my anger
or discouraged because of my discouragement
or frightened of my fears
or rejecting of my feelings of rejection.
I can live with them in peace
for I have seen that God can use them for my good.

I do the same
with some of the many other things about my life
that I want to change:
My body's disabilities . . .
My personal shortcomings . . .
The external circumstances of my life . . .
The happenings of the past . . .
The persons with whom I live . . .
The whole world as it is . . .
Old age, sickness, death.
I speak to them with love
and the consciousness that they somehow fit
into God's plan.

In doing so I undergo a transformation:
while everything about me is the same
—the world, my family, my feelings,
my body, my neuroses—
I am the same no longer.
I am more loving now,
more accepting of what is undesirable.
More peaceful, too,
for having come to see
that violence cannot lead to lasting change
—only love and understanding can.[5]

Praying the Chapter

Gracious and tender God,
I struggle to forgive and accept myself when I have hurt
others or when I have failed to live up to my spiritual ideals.
And I just can't seem to accept that the disturbing thoughts
and troubling feelings that I have from time to time are
an acceptable part of me, a part of me that
does not make me unacceptable to you.

Give me the strength and courage to name and own what
I have tended to resist, reject, and declare
unacceptable and unforgivable in myself.
Help me to not push these parts of myself "underground"
but to bring them out into the open where they will lose
some of their power over me as I begin to heal
in the deepest regions of my being.

I realize, Lord, that I need to take some regular action if I
hope to become more self-accepting and self-forgiving.
Give me the vision to see—and claim—my strengths, gifts,
and accomplishments rather than blindly scolding myself
for my weaknesses, limitations, and failures.
Free me from my tendency to compare myself
in a negative and hurtful manner to others.
And grace me with the wisdom to reach out to the
people in my life whose caring presence helps me
to love, accept, and forgive myself.

Teach me how to affirm myself just like I would a child for
the child within me is craving a kind and affirming word.
Be with me as I take on the ruthless voice of the inner critic.
Help me call upon my own inner voice of love, acceptance,
and forgiveness, as I join it with yours in a chorus

that will transform the voice of the inner critic into a
gentle, encouraging, self-advocating voice of
love, acceptance, and forgiveness.
Amen

For Reflection, Journaling, or Discussion

1. Of the seven suggested ways of growing in self-acceptance and self-forgiveness that were discussed, which ones appeal to you the most? Explain. If you were to add two or three additional suggestions, what would they be?

2. Who are the people who have been exceptionally accepting or forgiving of you at various points and stages in your life? You might recall these individuals in five- or ten-year increments, beginning with your childhood, teen years, twenties, thirties, and so on. Or you might focus on those who were accepting or forgiving of you during your most trying, challenging, or painful times.

3. Spend some time reflecting upon, journaling about, or discussing Anthony de Mello's "The Enlightenment." What in particular strikes you? What one or two phrases are especially comforting or encouraging to you at this point in your life? Explain.

CHAPTER 5

ACCEPTING AND FORGIVING
OTHERS—IMPERFECTLY

It is for us to make the effort.
The result is always in God's hands.
—Mahatma Gandhi

MUCH TO OUR PERSONAL AND COMMUNAL detriment, we have a tendency, both as individuals and as members of various groups and communities, to create a "me versus him or her" or "us versus them" mindset. Not only do we have a difficult time accepting or forgiving these "others," but at times we are prone to demonizing them—though we may not usually think of it in such strong terms. These "others" whom we struggle to accept, forgive, or sometimes demonize may be individuals who have hurt us in the recent or distant past. These "others" could also be an entire country or the leader of a country our nation is at odds with—or perhaps even a leader of our own country. Or these "others" might be a particular political, ethnic, religious, social, or professional group we disagree with, disapprove of, or, for whatever reasons, don't feel comfortable with.

The overwhelming majority of us can easily identify who these people are for ourselves by calling to mind the individuals and groups we would least like to go on a two-week vacation with. (Fundamentalist/ultra-conservative Christians are one such group for me.) But we sometimes forget that if we are to know a deeper and more abiding inner peace, these people may be the very ones we need to make a more concerted effort to accept or forgive as we de-demonize and rehumanize them in our hearts and minds.

Oftentimes we share some common ground with these "others." In my case I share a passion for God with Christian fundamentalists, though our understandings of the divine differ greatly. We also share the capacity to become rigid, for I sometimes become as inflexible in my theological viewpoints as many fundamentalists do in theirs. But even if you and I cannot recognize anything in common with those we deem "other," we all share the common ground of being vulnerable, flawed, interdependent human beings who share life on this fragile planet. And that is enough commonality, enough grounds for us to put forth the effort to accept and forgive each other more fully.

In this chapter we will explore some of the reasons why it can be so hard to accept and forgive certain individuals and groups. We will also consider how we might grow in the acceptance and forgiveness process, for high stakes are involved: our inner peace and happiness, which, of course, directly impacts the quality of our relationships with others. Our hope is to make a little bit—or perhaps a "lotta" bit—of progress so that we can enjoy the serenity that usually dissipates when we are unhappily stewing about, judging, resenting, or simply at odds with others.

Accepting and Forgiving Others— Imperfectly

Perhaps on occasion you have felt some guilt, as I have, for not being more accepting and forgiving of others. If you are a Christian, or if you subscribe to another religious or spiritual path, accepting and forgiving others is not only what we are supposed to *do* but who we are supposed to *be*. Jesus accepted and forgave others and invites us to do the same. But there are certain people I have tried to accept and forgive at various times in my life yet haven't been able to despite my best efforts. Even when I have entreated God with all my heart to help me forgive or accept a particular person, I have still failed, or at least it has *felt* like failure to me.

If you, too, have tried and seemingly failed upon occasion, I wonder if we are missing an essential, but as yet unidentified, component to our genetic makeup, perhaps a crucial DNA strand of acceptance or forgiveness. Or maybe your or my periodic struggle to accept and forgive others is simply a painful part of what it means to be a fallible, sometimes conflicted, human being. Part of us wants to move toward being more forgiving and accepting of others, while another part of us resists any such movement. In fact, as soon as I make any conscious attempts to forgive or accept a particular person or group, my desire to *not* forgive or accept often grows stronger and more intense—at least initially—which can be very discouraging.

Pause, Ponder, or Practice

Have you ever struggled with these conflicting, perhaps even seesawing, desires to forgive and accept someone and to not forgive and accept this person? If so, explain. When we are either not wanting or not ready to forgive or accept the "other," we sometimes feel guilt or shame because an inner voice may be telling us that we should be doing both. What might you say to this voice? How can you treat yourself gently when you are neither willing nor ready to forgive or accept a particular person or group?

Maybe if you and I just ignore this unforgivable or unacceptable person or group and go about our daily business, the hurt that we have experienced or the dislike—even the hatred or contempt—we feel, will just go away. But it usually doesn't. Resentments revisit us at all hours of the day and night and in all sorts of settings. I could be surrounded by the Dali Lama, Mother Teresa, Mahatma Gandhi, and a host of heavenly angels, and still be suddenly swept away by an unsolicited and unwanted feeling of resentment when a memory of how someone has hurt me, perhaps decades ago, arises. In another book, I probed the difficulty of overcoming our resentments.

> Despite our best efforts to forgive and move on, resentments tend to resurface again and again. It's almost as if they have a life of their own and don't want us to ever forgive our offenders! Resentments re-send to our conscious awareness specific memories of how we have been hurt in the recent or distant past. We may feel intense hatred as we fantasize disturbing scenes of retribution. And then shame or guilt may torment us for even having such thoughts and feelings—especially if we are trying to live as spiritual people.[1]

So is our desire to become more accepting and forgiving of others hopeless? Are we bound to fail regardless of our efforts? No, but making some progress, however slight, and regaining a measure of inner peace, however small, falls well within the realm of what is possible. Progress is attainable while perfection is not. Perfection—

complete and constant unconditional love, acceptance, and forgiveness of others—may be the ideal that inspires us; imperfection—incomplete and fluctuating love, acceptance, and forgiveness of others—is the reality that requires us to keep at it.

As people who are trying to live, rather than just talk about, our spiritual or religious values, we never accept or forgive or love or have faith or most anything else to the fullest extent possible, and certainly not perfectly. We need to accept, not just once but over and over again, that our attempts to forgive and accept certain others, as was mentioned a moment ago, are frequently going to be met with conflicting and powerful desires to do neither. Such self-acceptance will free us from feeling like we have failed, provide us with the perspective to see that it is a spiral-like process, and empower us to continue or renew our efforts to accept and forgive others more completely.

Our sense of inner peace, however, is usually going to be quite weak, maybe even temporarily absent, during those times when we are feeling most resentful and unforgiving of others. But the very good news is that it will grow stronger, or perhaps return to us in spades, as we make some effort, even a modest, conflicted, and hesitant one, to accept and forgive someone(s) a little more fully.

Being at an inner place in which we are absolutely unwilling to accept or forgive is nothing to be ashamed of, because we don't struggle to accept or forgive other people just for a challenge or for something to do. Rather, our struggle can be attributed to a variety of interconnected and complex factors including our personality, our unique issues, the extent of our wounds, and our upbringing. Our challenge is to not become too entrenched in a state of complete unwillingness to forgive or accept the "other," which is possible as you and I practice some of the forthcoming suggestions in this chapter and call upon the skills and wisdom we have acquired elsewhere.

Our Reluctance to Forgive and Accept Others

Let's begin by honestly admitting that we sometimes don't want to forgive or accept some people. In fact, let's say it: "I don't *want* to forgive or accept some people!" Now let's insert the specific individuals and groups that, at this point in our lives, we do not want to accept or forgive. "I don't want to forgive or accept (name)." Candidly admitting our reluctance, even our complete unwillingness, to forgive or accept a particular person or group is a crucial first step toward getting out of the unhappy prison in which we are being beaten up by feelings of hatred, contempt, or resentment. This unseen prison within also houses our judgmental and condemning tendencies, which, if left unchecked, also leave us feeling unhappy and peaceless.

It is indeed ironic that we often hold the keys to this inner prison and can walk out at any time without obtaining the permission of a parole board, but we sometimes prefer to stay captive to these extremely unpleasant feelings and painful states of mind. Perhaps like those who have spent many years in prison and are leery of reentering the outside world once again, we, too, may be feeling apprehensive about leaving the familiar, albeit unhappy, confines of our unaccepting and resentment-prone hearts and minds. We want to get out, but we may have lived with our resentments or our refusal to accept or forgive certain others for such a long time, that we also want to stay in our lifeless inner prison. We long to get out of prison without giving up what keeps us prisoners. We aspire to be free of the inner discord that accompanies our refusal to accept or forgive someone without having to accept or forgive this person. On occasion we might stick the key in the lock, open the door, and take one step out—or maybe even a few steps—only to rush back in, slam the door, and curl up on our lonely, lumpy cot in the corner.

Jesus came to give life and to set people free in so many ways. He disclosed an understanding of God that grew out of his Jewish heritage but that also went beyond it. He revealed a God who is totally for us, which freed people then and now from a narrow religious legalism in which we try, in vain, to gain favor with a God who already favors and accepts us, and who is wholeheartedly committed to our well being. And he taught us the best way to live our lives.

Many of his teachings about how to live are found in Matthew 5–7, the Sermon on the Mount. Included among his instructions, he urges us to go the extra mile, give to those in need, do not worry about the future, love your enemies, do not judge others, do not take revenge, and pray for and forgive those who have wronged you. What's striking about these teachings is that they are the best way for us to live, as well as beneficial to others. They are often good for others, although I can forgive someone who is no longer in my life and this person will probably not know that I have forgiven him or her, but they are always good for me! Forgiving this person sets me free from acute or lingering resentments. When I, with massive "doses" of God's grace, am able to forgive someone else, I am happier and more at peace. When I refrain from returning a hurt for a hurt received, I not only don't have to deal with the inevitable aftermath of guilt and shame, but the other person does not suffer a new wound from me because I acted upon my vengeful urges. The hurt-retaliation cycle gets stopped, even if only on a relatively small scale and only temporarily, for I may, in a moment of weakness, not resist the temptation to return an offense tomorrow.

Toward Fuller—not Perfect—Acceptance and Forgiveness of Others

The following thoughts and suggestions are meant to help you and me accept and forgive more comprehensively (though still imperfectly) the specific people and groups we either reject or resent. Our goal is to reclaim or restore our inner peace, which is critically dependent upon the efforts we make to accept and forgive others more completely. Behind the scenes is our God of peace who is with us and is empowering us every step of the way.

Accepting and forgiving others, very much like grief, is often a messy and many-layered process. I wish it were as simple as steps one, two, three, and we're done, but it's usually not, especially when we are dealing with our most recent hurts or our deeper wounds from yesteryear as well as our most powerful urges to flat out reject and condemn others. In fact, we might feel like we have indeed accepted or forgiven someone, only to discover at a later date that we have cleared away but the first of several layers, and our sense of inner peace at the time, though well deserved, was simply a temporary reprieve. As the hurtful memories resurface or as the judgmental or hateful thoughts and feelings return, we may dishearteningly surmise that we have made no progress, but we have. We simply have more work to do, which, of course, is hardly simple at all; in fact, it's often among the most challenging work we will ever do.

Perhaps the messy and multi-layered nature of this process might be captured by an image of a rain-soaked, muddy hill we must climb in order to forgive. We slip and slide as we grasp and claw our way to the top. When we finally get there, perhaps emotionally and spiritually drained, a refreshing pool of water and clean, dry clothes await us as the sun beams warmly upon us. The path is now smooth and level with no hills in sight. An exhilarating sense of harmony and inner peace swells our hearts, and our minds may be pleasantly dumbfounded by the timeless, if ephemeral, realization that we really are all one after all! We continue lightly and effortlessly along our way, but then, without any warning, another rainy and muddy hill appears that we must climb. And so the forgiveness process continues.

Pause, Ponder, or Practice

If the forgiveness process is indeed a bit messy like grieving, what are some of the stages we must go through? For example, "anger" or "unwillingness to accept or forgive" or "I will forgive only if he or she asks for my forgiveness" might constitute such stages. Have you ever felt like you had completely accepted and forgiven someone only to discover another layer of angry and hurt feelings rising unexpectedly again? If so, explain.

Forgiving others does not mean that the hurt we have experienced at their hands is okay, discountable, or excusable. Judy Logue, in her short, practical, and user-friendly book, *Forgiving the People You Love to Hate,* emphasizes that forgiveness "is not approval. It is not immediate restoration of trust. It is not canceling of consequences. . . . Forgiveness does not begin with 'It's okay. Just forget it.'"[2]

While it is possible to dwell excessively upon our injuries, and perhaps on at least one occasion most of us have read—actually misread—evil or hurtful intent when there was none, we also don't want to dismiss or discount our pain and try to forgive too soon. We strive to neither magnify nor minimize our hurts. We seek to neither prematurely canonize nor permanently demonize our offenders. We try to walk the wide middle way between these two extremes.

For some of us, and this may be especially true of many women who have learned to suppress their anger, the unhealthy extreme we lean toward is the one in which we discount or dismiss our hurts and too readily excuse those who have mistreated us. And by quickly excusing, we fail to honor and trust our own experiences, feelings, and perceptions, which is peace-robbing in and of itself.

We can make efforts to accept and forgive others, even if they refuse to make any efforts to accept or forgive us. We can take the first step, even when the other person is more at fault than we are or even when he or she is totally culpable. We make efforts to accept and forgive the "other," not only because our religious or spiritual values call us to, but more importantly, because our inner peace is at stake. We want our serenity back, which will begin to return to us as we embark—sometimes alone—on the high and narrow road that Jesus says leads to life.

The Buddhist monk and teacher Thich Nhat Hanh reminds us that we share much in common with the person we may be trying to forgive: our wounded humanity.

> Our enemy is not the other person, no matter what he or she has done. If we look deeply into ourselves, we can see that their act was a manifestation of our

collective consciousness. We are all filled with violence, hatred, and fear, so why blame someone whose upbringing was without love or understanding? When you look deeply into your anger, you will see that the person you call your enemy is also suffering. As soon as you see that, the capacity of accepting and having compassion for him is there. Jesus called this "loving your enemy." When you are able to love your enemy, he or she is no longer your enemy. The idea of "enemy" vanishes and is replaced by the notion of someone who is suffering and needs your compassion.[3]

We may need to enter more deeply into our thoughts and feelings of hatred, contempt, judgmentalism, anger, resentment, and so on, in order to rise out of them, in order to better forgive or accept the other person or group and regain our inner peace. Allowing ourselves to fully experience these painful—perhaps even violent—thoughts and feelings is a tremendously difficult thing to do. But if we implode, so to speak, and allow these thoughts and feelings to burst inside us, perhaps by writing an undeliverable angry letter or by finding some type of physical release, we overcome a significant portion of the obstacle to inner and interpersonal peace. Too often we try to prematurely shut these thoughts and feelings down, which only causes them to grow stronger. We say to ourselves such things as "I shouldn't be thinking this way" or "I shouldn't be feeling this way" or "This isn't very Christian or very spiritual." But maybe if we just write that angry letter or scream or yell in order to release steam or go for a walk or punch that pillow or punching bag, inner peace will return to us more quickly.

We can implode in a multitude of ways that do not hurt others or ourselves. I have found that occasionally punching the punching bag that is hanging in our laundry room frees me from the hatred and violence I feel toward someone, and much to my surprise, has actually been instrumental to my being able to (eventually) see the other person with eyes of compassion. For me, the road to compassion, as well as to acceptance and forgiveness of the "other," is sometimes through my punching bag as I release my anger energy. Releasing the intensity of these feelings of violence, hatred, and fear that Thich Nhat Hahn says we all have, helps me get to the point where I can "look deeply" into my anger and into the other person and rediscover compassion for both of us. And when I don't let my troubling thoughts and feelings out in healthy ways, I usually don't end up with compassion for the other person or inner peace for myself.

Maintaining emotional or physical distance from certain people with whom we have been in relationship results in an increased sense of dis-ease, alienation, and suspicion, whereas reconnecting with the "other" may lead to the dropping of our guard and to the restoration of inner and interpersonal peace. Who are these people that we are called to be in relationship with? Each one of us has to determine who that might be for ourselves. It may include our family of origin as well as some of our friends and colleagues. However, it is not uncommon for adult siblings—and friends and colleagues for that matter—to become estranged from each other as they grow in different directions over the years, not just geographically but in a number of much more significant ways including lifestyle, religious and political beliefs, and values. And sometimes conflicts occur from time to time, even between adult siblings or between grown children and their parents, and as was mentioned in chapter 3, most of us have emergent and fragile rather than highly developed and resilient conflict resolution skills.

If we have become estranged from someone, whether a member of our family or a friend or colleague, or if we have been maintaining our distance and have become suspicious of the "other," we may regain a sense of inner peace as we make an effort to reconnect. When we walk away from a relationship without attempting to reconcile and reestablish some common ground or without bringing some closure if the former is not possible, our inner peace tends to walk away from us.

Sometimes for the sake of our own inner peace we may need to terminate a relationship—even with a family member—or set strong boundaries around a relationship in which certain topics or events from the past are simply off limits. Psychologist Terry D. Cooper says that we have every right to protect our boundaries and that boundary violation is always dysfunctional even if it is done out of a sense of religious or moral conviction or superiority.[4] We may have simply grown in a different direction, perhaps a different spiritual or religious direction, and we need others to respect our path, even if they disagree with it, if the relationship is going to continue. Or we may simply hold less in common with this person than we did at a previous stage of our lives, and so our contact with each other may naturally be less frequent as a result.

Perhaps most of us have heard about or even know certain people who did not become reconciled with each other until one of them was on his or her deathbed. Our challenge is to not wait so long. If we continue to dismiss or ignore these certain "others" or cut them off because of our anger, hurt, or fear rather than embark on the risky but potentially rewarding road toward reconciling or resolving whatever has come between us, we place our inner peace at risk. Generally speaking, I believe that as we open our-selves up to reconciliation or resolution, the potential rewards of inner peace outweigh the risks of further estrangement. Oftentimes, the hurts and suspicions and fears dissolve as we reconnect with the "other," and we may even delight in getting to know each other once again.

Memories of hurts will surface from time to time, and along with these painful memories may come feelings of anger or resentment. But these memories and feelings do not necessarily mean that we have failed to forgive or accept the other person. What is so confusing and troubling to many of us is that we may have worked really hard to forgive some-one, yet these painful feelings still surface from time to time. As a result, we doubt ourselves and feel like we have totally failed in our attempts to forgive. But that is not the case.

We can rest assured that we have made substantial progress along the imperfect and messy process of forgiv-ing the other person when two signs are present. First, the memories and accompanying painful emotions are resur-facing less often than they used to, and when they do arise they are relatively short-lived. We don't resist the memory but try to flow with it, as we allow ourselves to feel some intensely uncomfortable feelings such as hatred or anger once again. Then when the memory has spent itself—and it will—we let it go and get back to the business at hand within a relatively short period of time, perhaps within just a few minutes.

Second, the wound that we suffered has not held us back from carrying on with our lives. We have chosen to be fully responsible for the rest of our lives despite the hurt that we suf-fered earlier in our lives. We have not succumbed to the temptation of being a victim. If we are experiencing these painful memories and feelings more frequently and are struggling to let go of the past and move on with our lives, we may have some more work to do. It does not mean that we have failed to forgive or accept the other person, but that we need more time and healing. Each person has his or her own unique forgiveness and acceptance timetable. Mine is slug-like slow; be sure to always trust yours! Scolding ourselves for not being further along does not help us to progress any faster. Self-compassion and self-gentleness are what's needed when we get stuck in the forgiveness and acceptance process.

As we struggle to forgive and accept certain individuals and groups, the success of our efforts is dependent upon our willingness to try to refrain from judging and condemning them. As much as possible, we want to focus on the other person's or group's behavior that has hurt us or that we are struggling to accept, and not get into making wholesale judgments and condemnations about who they are as people. Terry Cooper, in his exceptionally wise and helpful book *I'm Judgmental You're Judgmental*, expresses this so clearly:

> It is an arrogant illusion that we can "size up" someone's entire life. . . . Perhaps one of the reasons Jesus warned so rigorously against judgmentalism is that it makes a "god" or "idol" of our own viewpoint. . . . We don't know how someone has been hurt, the struggles of their life, the overall context out of which they have lived. Some may think this sounds dangerously close to "excusing" another's behavior, but this is not at all what I am suggesting. I am simply saying that we, coming out of our own set of assumptions, viewpoints, limitations, and cognitive finitude, cannot possibly deliver a "final verdict" about another's *entire* life. We

may have very definite judgments about specific *acts*
this person has committed. But we just don't have the
intellectual resources to determine the nature of his or
her entire existence.[5]

Refraining from judging and condemning is extremely
difficult to do. Being judgmental requires absolutely nothing of us and we all do it at times, whereas making sound
judgments calls for a much more delicate touch, disci-
plined mind, and generous heart. Judging and condemning others is a great deal easier than forgiving and
accepting them. But maybe if we recall that we would want
others to refrain from making wholesale judgments and
condemnations about who we are as a person when we
have acted poorly, we, too, can extend the same grace and
benefit of the doubt to others. And if we are ever feeling
morally superior to someone or looking down upon
someone whose behavior is falling short, we might pray
the prayer that a wise mentor in my life taught me: God,
forgive me for the times I have (engaged in that same
behavior or in a different one that has also been hurtful or
destructive).

Such a prayer reminds us that we are not superior to all
the "moral inferiors" out there in the world. Such a prayer
reminds us that we, too, fall short and hurt others and that
on our better days, as the Twelve-Step saying suggests,
"there by the grace of God go I." Such a prayer helps us see
the struggling "other" with eyes of compassion. Such a
prayer is akin to that of the tax collector in Luke's Gospel.
Unlike the Pharisee who thanked God because he was not
like the morally inferior, the tax collector refused to look
heavenward, but instead beat his breast and pleaded, "God,
be merciful to me, a sinner" (Luke 18:11-13).

Pause, Ponder, or Practice

How do you rein in your judgmental or condemnatory tendencies? When do you tend to be most judgmental? When are you least judgmental? I am most prone to judging and condemning others when I am being judgmental and condemning of myself. Do you experience a correlation between your judging of others and your judging of yourself? Explain. Try praying the prayer mentioned above when you catch yourself judging and condemning others: "God, forgive me for the times I have (name the hurtful behavior)."

God is with us in our struggles to forgive and accept others and will help us; we do not have to do this difficult work alone. If there is ever a time in life when we need the grace and power of God, it is when we are trying to forgive and accept those individuals and groups who have hurt us or who we look down on. Sometimes our tendency may be to think that God loves us more when we are accepting and forgiving these people than when we are rejecting and condemning them, but that is not the case. God's love for us is unconditional. We can't earn it by forgiving and accepting others and we can't unearn it or lose God's love by resenting and rejecting them.

Our God is with us no matter how deeply and powerfully our feelings of hatred, resentment, anger, and the like run. Our God embraces us when we get stuck in the process, helps us up when we are ready to try again, picks us up and encourages us when we falter, and accompanies us each and every step and stage of the way. Our God is a God of acceptance, forgiveness, and reconciliation, and will help us to accept, forgive, and, when possible, become reconciled with the "other," for it is both God's nature and God's work in the world.

We can turn over to God for temporary or long-term care those whom we are not ready, willing, or able to forgive or accept at this point in our lives, for our acceptance and forgiveness "tanks" may be temporarily empty. And we can count on God to lead us to "wounded healers"—friends, counselors, pastors, rabbis, or spiritual directors—who will be able to help us process our deeper wounds and experience a greater degree of healing, along with acceptance and forgiveness for the "other" and inner peace for ourselves.

In the next chapter we will look more closely at the unconditional nature of God's acceptance and forgiveness. We will also examine why it is so difficult for many of us to believe in such a wildly gracious God, and identify a few ways that can help us experience God's love, acceptance, and forgiveness more deeply.

Praying the Chapter

Loving God,
you expect way, way, way too much of me
when you ask me to accept and forgive others.
Yes, for the most part I am pretty good
at accepting friends, loved ones, and
people who think and talk and act like me.
But when it comes to accepting others, especially
those who are truly "other," those who do not
hold the same beliefs and values that I do,
well, we run into major problems.
And then when it comes to forgiving those who
have hurt me deeply and, come to think of it,
even not so deeply, I just can't seem to do it.

But maybe your acceptance and forgiveness expectations
are high because you have even higher hopes for me, hopes that
I will be happy and know a greater measure of inner peace,
both of which are dependent upon my efforts
to accept and forgive others.

Be patient with me as I make some hesitant and conflicted efforts
to accept and forgive my sisters and brothers more fully.
I know it is a messy, many-layered process, so perhaps I really need
to pray for the grace to be patient with myself.

Help me to remember that accepting and forgiving those who have
hurt me does not mean that what they did or said was okay.
Give me the courage to enter fully into my painful feelings
of hatred and anger and resentment so that their power
over me might be decreased and my sense of
inner peace might, in turn, be increased.
And when I struggle to accept or forgive the "other,"
be with me as I try, and too often fail, to avoid
the slippery slopes of judgmentalism and condemnation,
for only you know the inner workings—and hidden wounds—
of each person's heart including mine.

Finally, may I always remember that you are
with me always, even when I get stuck in resentment
or when I am keeping my distance from someone or when
I am judging and condemning someone or when
I am remembering a wound from long ago and suffer
some temporary feelings of hatred and anger all over again.
For your love, acceptance, and forgiveness,
amazingly enough, are not dependent upon how well
I love, accept, and forgive others, and for that
I am so very grateful.
Amen

For Reflection, Journaling, or Discussion

1. How have you grown in your ability to accept individuals and groups who have been difficult for you to accept? What challenges do you still encounter? Have you ever prayed for the grace to accept those who are different from you just as they are? Do you think that praying for this grace could help you accept the "other" more fully? Explain.

2. Do you think that separating a person's behavior from who they are as a person can help you in your attempts to forgive those who have hurt you? Explain. Be willing to share with others whatever helps you to forgive more fully.

3. How do you handle painful memories when they resurface, especially when you have truly tried to forgive the other person? Does it make sense that these memories do not mean that you have failed to forgive the "other" and that, like our more pleasant memories, will simply surface from time to time? Why or why not?

CHAPTER 6

ACCEPTING GOD'S LOVE, ACCEPTANCE, AND FORGIVENESS

> Put on your jumping shoes, and jump
> into the heart of God.
>
> —Meister Eckhart

LINKED TO OUR STRUGGLES TO LOVE AND accept and forgive both ourselves and others is the difficulty many of us have believing that we are truly loved, accepted, and forgiven by God. Because we tend to be most accepting of ourselves when we are speaking and acting in an "acceptable" manner, it can be incredibly hard to believe that God accepts us even when—and perhaps especially when—our words and actions fall far short of the mark. Surely God must love us more on those days when we love others than on the days when we seem to be incapable of such love. Surely God must deem us to be more acceptable when we are accepting of others rather than when we are busily judging and condemning them. Surely God must find it easier to forgive us when we are forgiving those who have hurt us rather than when we are clinging to resentments as if they were life itself.

In short, we tend to shrink God to our size and either consciously or subconsciously expect God to respond to us in the little, petty, and perhaps even tit for tat ways that we so frequently respond to each other. Because other people are more likely to love us when we are acting in lovable ways, we doubt that God can love us when we are at our most unlovable. Because other people tend to accept us when we haven't strayed too far outside the parameters of what is considered to be acceptable, we expect God's acceptance of us to be bound by similar limitations. And because other people are more likely to forgive us if we don't keep failing in the same areas, we expect that God's forgiveness is dependent upon our ability to overcome the particular bad habit, sin, or temptation that is plaguing us.

Most of us have probably experienced conditional types of acceptance and approval from ourselves and from others many more times during the course of our lives than unconditional acceptance and approval. As a general rule, we were most unconditionally loved and accepted during our infancy, which we don't remember—though perhaps we do at some wordless level of our being—and as we grew older, more conditions were attached to the love and acceptance we received from others. Now as adults, we really don't expect others, including those closest to us, to love and accept us without any conditions; we feel that we have to earn or deserve it, at least to some degree.

As a result of lifelong "conditioning," of being accepted and valued on a conditional basis, many of us haven't really experienced God as one whose love, acceptance, and forgiveness are totally unconditional, without any conditions at all. And that which we haven't experienced—or perhaps have experienced only on rare occasions—is much more difficult to believe in and trust than what has been prevalent in our lives.

In this chapter, we will continue our probe into why it can be so difficult for many of us—perhaps all of us at certain times in our lives—to accept the reality that God loves and accepts and forgives us as we are. We will also explore the nature of God's unconditional love and acceptance, which can come to us in a variety of ways, particularly through those special people who have been most accepting and forgiving of us. Lastly, we will consider a few tangible ways to "jump into the heart of God," especially when we are feeling unworthy of being caught and embraced by the one whose heart and arms are always open to receive us. Our hope is to be able to experience God's love, acceptance, and forgiveness in those most unlovable, unacceptable, and unforgivable regions of our being which we have declared undeserving of such lavish and reckless grace, and as a result, enjoy the priceless gift of inner peace once again.

Why We Sometimes Struggle to Accept God's Love, Acceptance, and Forgiveness

Because we have unique personalities and experiences in life, the reasons why each of us may struggle at different times to accept God's love, acceptance, and forgiveness are likely to have a uniquely personal element to them. Yet one or more of the following five reasons or factors might be held in common by many of us.

As already mentioned, when we withhold love, acceptance, and forgiveness from ourselves, and when others offer a conditional type of love, acceptance, and forgiveness based upon our behavior or performance, it makes it difficult to believe in, much less to accept, God's unconditional love, acceptance, and forgiveness. We seldom offer ourselves unconditional love and acceptance.

To test whether or not this is true, the next time you fail or fall short as a parent, spouse, at the workplace, or in some other aspect of your life, notice which inner voice arises first and is more dominant: the critical one or the accepting and forgiving one. (Some of us may not even be aware that we have an inner voice of acceptance and forgiveness, perhaps because we have seldom called upon it to speak its truth!) Are you able to see your moment of failure *as* a moment of failure or does it negatively impact how you see and value yourself *as* a person?

And when it comes to how others love and accept us, we experience the whole gamut from instant rejection, to conditional and performance-based acceptance, to those rare persons who love and accept us for who we are as human beings even when we are at our worst. The latter somehow have a way of simultaneously loving and accepting us while holding us accountable when our behavior is out of line. While we treasure these special people in our lives, some type of condition, usually unspoken, is attached to the way that many, if not most, individuals and groups accept us. Thus, we make the assumption that God, too, has conditions and standards and performance expectations we must meet if we are to be the recipients of divine love, acceptance, and forgiveness.

We may expect too much of ourselves at times and because we are not able to live up to what psychologists call our "idealized self," we make the incorrect assumption that God must feel as disappointed with us as we sometimes do with ourselves. There is a fine line between trying to improve the way we live out our spiritual ideals and becoming captive to an unattainable idealized self. We all have the notion of an idealized self that we must rein in from time to time. If I were able to live out my idealized self, I would never get angry, much less express anger in an inappropriate manner. I would also never be afraid, and I would pretty much deal with all of life's challenges and obstacles with incredible class and equanimity. But in my real life, I do get angry and don't always handle it as well as I would like, I do feel afraid at times, and I usually don't face life's challenging and upsetting moments with a calm sense of detachment.

What's rather amazing, when I stop to think about it, is that I feel disappointed with myself each and every time I fail to live up to my idealized self. I feel disappointed with myself when I feel angry or afraid or judgmental and decide that I have once again failed in my attempt to follow the way that Jesus teaches us to live. Perhaps you have experienced a similar sense of self-disappointment in an area of ongoing struggle as well. And then you and I may assume that God must also be disappointed with us and that God isn't really going to accept us until our idealized self becomes a reality—which, of course, isn't going to happen. And so we struggle to accept that God could possibly love and accept and forgive us as we are, as real people with flaws and weaknesses rather than as ideal people.

Pause, Ponder, or Practice

What would you be like if you were able to live out your idealized self? What do you struggle with in your real life that you would no longer be struggling with if you were able to live out your idealized self? What difference is there, if any, between the idealized self and the perfect self? Would life be more interesting or less interesting if we were all able to live out our idealized selves? Explain.

Because most of us have struggled, perhaps with little or no sense of progress, to overcome some of our most persistent shortcomings, weaknesses, and bad habits, we feel unworthy of accepting God's love, acceptance, and forgiveness. Again, we are back to having to perform well so that we might earn what is freely given. Because *we* have such a difficult time accepting some of these reprehensible, what we may even consider to be shameful, areas of personal struggle, we believe that *God* must also struggle to accept and forgive us when we have failed to overcome a particular weakness for the one-millionth time.

I once heard a sermon in which the priest said that most of us confess the same sins again and again. It was such a welcome relief for me to hear these words because I thought that I was the only one who was unable to overcome these chronic "sins" and shortcomings. Because we keep these wounded aspects of ourselves so well hidden from others, we assume that we are unique in failing to overcome them, but we are not. Hence, the good news is twofold. First, the overwhelming majority of us face a few areas of ongoing struggle, so you and I are not moral anomalies when we experience recurring setbacks. Second, God is with us in the struggle, always offering us love, acceptance, and forgiveness with the hope that we, in turn, will offer love, acceptance, and forgiveness to ourselves.

We struggle to accept God's acceptance and forgiveness because sin and sinfulness are sometimes overemphasized in the Christian tradition. This is not to say that they should be eliminated from Christianity, because the effects of personal, social, and systemic sin are truly devastating. But in my opinion, when sin and sinfulness are emphasized to the point where we lose sight of our God-given goodness and we fail to hear the call to be incarnate cocreators of divine love in the world, then we need to restore some theological balance. If we get too hung up on our sinfulness, it may prevent us from knowing the peace that comes from experiencing God's acceptance.

Our first identity is not as sinners; rather, our first identity is as children of God. We are "fearfully and wonderfully made" (Ps. 139:14) in the image of a loving, accepting, and forgiving creator. Those of us who are parents make every effort to accept and forgive our children, and God, whose parent-like qualities exceed ours by unimaginable exponential proportions, accepts and forgives us.

Some of us might need to reclaim a sense of our God-given goodness—even though we all sin and fall short of the mark. And in order to balance the confession of sin that is an integral part of many church liturgies, maybe we would be wise to include a statement of faith that points to our first identity as children of a loving, accepting, and forgiving God. Such a statement might read something like the one below.

A Statement of Faith in Our First Identity

We are, first and foremost, children of God. We are made in the very image of our loving, accepting, and forgiving Creator.

Made in God's image, we are called to reflect divine love and to be agents of divine love in our lives, in the lives of others, and throughout the world.

Because God accepts us *as we are*, we are called and commissioned to accept ourselves and others as we are so that we might become *more* than we are.

Though we sin and fall short of the mark as individuals and communities, God forgives us without condition and without end. Set free from guilt and shame, we are invited each day and each moment to walk with the Spirit in the paths of life, light, and love.

Knowing that such love and acceptance and forgiveness are always extended to us, we, in turn, offer unconditional love, acceptance, and forgiveness to ourselves, especially when we are most wounded and painfully cognizant of our shortcomings.

We also extend unconditional love, acceptance, and forgiveness to others, especially when they are most wounded and regardless of whether or not they are cognizant of their shortcomings, so that we might be saved from judging and condemning them for having flaws and weaknesses and struggles in life just like us.

We are, first and foremost, children of God. We are made in the very image of our loving, accepting, and forgiving Creator.

Thanks be to God. Amen

We struggle to accept God's acceptance and forgiveness because we often deny our negative shadow and exile our painful emotions. This ties into our idealized self that we addressed a moment ago. Though we are made in the Creator's image, we all have troubling thoughts (our negative shadow) and painful emotions that we struggle to accept in ourselves. Our negative shadow is alive and well when we are focusing on *other* people's weaknesses and shortcomings, weaknesses and shortcomings that are also present in us to some degree. When we are tearing down another person, we are often tearing down something that is in us as well, though we may deny it because it is too painful or shameful to acknowledge.

When we attempt to deny our negative shadow and cast out our painful emotions, we become ever more fragmented and peaceless. And because it is not possible to rid ourselves of either our negative shadow or our painful emotions, we suffer every time they surface in our lives. Feelings of hatred, judgmentalism, jealousy, anger, self-righteousness, intolerance, pettiness and the like are extremely hard to accept in ourselves. And because we struggle to accept that these shadowy elements and painful emotions are a part of us that are crying out for integration, some of us struggle to believe that God could, or would, accept us when they are fully operative.

The Nature of God's Unconditional Love, Acceptance, and Forgiveness

We would be wise to remember that which we tend to forget: God is God and not one of us. And so the "limitless lover" is not bound by our limitations, weaknesses, and character flaws, though they have the potential to bind—and trouble—us. God is totally "other" in the best sense of the word, in that the infinite nature of God's love, acceptance, and forgiveness as well as a host of other qualities such as compassion, commitment, and creativity are way beyond our finite human capacity to comprehend. The passionate prophets and poets of the Bible point to the magnanimous, "great-souled" nature of God including God's relentless and inexhaustible capacity to love, accept, and forgive us. The four passages below are among the hundreds and hundreds of biblical passages that attempt to convey what is inherently ineffable and much too deep for words.

"Do not fear, for I have redeemed you; I have called you by name, you are mine. . . . You are precious in my sight, and honored, and I love you. . . ."

   —Isa. 43:1b, 4a

"Can a woman forget her nursing child, or show no compassion for the child of her womb? Even these may forget, yet I will not forget you. See, I have inscribed you on the palms of my hands. . . ."

   —Isa. 49:15-16a

"God is merciful and gracious, slow to anger and abounding in steadfast love. . . . God does not deal with us according to our sins . . . as far as the east is from the west, so far God removes our transgressions from us."

   —Ps. 103:8, 10a, 12 (Oxford AIV)

"For it was you who formed my inward parts; you knit me together in my mother's womb . . . I am fearfully and wonderfully made."

   —Ps. 139:13-14a (Oxford AIV)

The God of the Bible, of both the Old and New Testaments, is one who is relentlessly relational. We cannot cut ourselves off from God's love, acceptance, and forgiveness no matter how unlovable, unacceptable, or unforgivable we may suppose ourselves to be.

When Jesus lived on earth, he never told people to change first so that he might accept them (although he was quite stern at times and became angry with both his disciples and some of the religious authorities). Instead, he always accepted the sinner, the outcast, and the rejected ones as they were. And as a result of being accepted and forgiven so completely and unconditionally, many, according to the Gospels, did indeed make some positive changes in their lives. But the acceptance came first and was not dependent upon any promise to try to change for the better. Perhaps the story of Jesus and Zacchaeus portrays as well as any other the unconditional and relational nature of divine love and its potential life-changing power.

> Jesus entered Jericho and was passing through it. A man named Zacchaeus was there, a chief tax collector who was rich. He was trying to see who Jesus was, but on account of the crowd he could not, because he was short in stature. So Zacchaeus ran ahead and climbed a sycamore tree to see Jesus, who was going to pass that way. When Jesus came to the place, he looked up and said to him, "Zacchaeus, hurry and come down; for I must stay at your house today." So he hurried down and was happy to welcome Jesus. All who saw it began to grumble and said, "Jesus has gone to be the guest of one who is a sinner." Zacchaeus stood there and said to Jesus, "Look, half of my possessions I will give to those who are poor; and if I have defrauded anyone of anything, I will pay back four times as much." Then Jesus said to him, "Today salvation has come to this house, because he too is a son of Sarah and Abraham. For the Human One came to seek out and to save the lost."
> —Luke 19:1-10 (Oxford AIV)

Though the story does not tell us directly, we can assume that Zacchaeus, because he was a hated tax collector, suffered from the pain of societal rejection and yearned for acceptance. Perhaps Jesus was able to recognize Zacchaeus's silent cry for acceptance and forgiveness when they made eye contact with each other.

Many of us are like Zacchaeus in that we long to experience divine acceptance and forgiveness more deeply and fully than we have to date. God invites us to come down from our trees, from our hiding places, and to know the peace that comes from being unconditionally loved, accepted, and forgiven. Sometimes our inner critical voice is like the crowd who grumbled that Jesus was going to dine at the house of a sinner. We may feel unworthy to turn our face toward the one whose face is always turned toward us, but we don't have to let our feelings run the show. We can turn to God in prayer even though we may, at times, feel unworthy of divine love, acceptance, and forgiveness. Roberta Bondi writes:

> We must set aside any idea that we must be in a good or holy frame of mind in the presence of God. We must be willing to pray when we feel mean or distracted or seriously tempted and even have the intention of giving in to the temptation. We must place ourselves trustfully or distrustfully in God's presence exactly as we are. We must relate to God in our prayer with our whole selves, and not only with our good parts.[1]

Our God desires to commune with us as we are, no matter what our sin, no matter what our frame of mind, no matter how disgusted we are with ourselves, and no matter how many times we have failed to overcome a particular weakness, bad habit, compulsion, or addiction. Our God desires that we approach the divine with our wounds so that we can be anointed with the healing balm of divine compassion, for our wounds and deep-seated woundedness are of special concern to the one who is compassion. Our God desires that we grow in our ability to accept the incomprehensible and healing truth that we are accepted, completely accepted, unconditionally accepted, *as we are*. And as a result of coming to know in the deepest regions of our heart that we are loved, accepted, and forgiven, we can begin to leave behind—perhaps not once and for all but bit by bit—those destructive behavior patterns that are hurtful to us or to others. Let's now turn our attention to a few ways that can help us accept divine love, acceptance, and forgiveness.

Five Suggestions to Help Us Accept God's Love, Acceptance, and Forgiveness

Because God's presence permeates creation, we can look for signs of divine love, acceptance, and forgiveness in the world around us. And, as was discussed in earlier chapters, we can exercise our God-given creativity by experimenting with rituals, affirmations, and exercises to help us in the acceptance and forgiveness process. The following suggestions are specifically intended to help you and me drop our resistance to being fully accepted and forgiven as we are and, as a result, know a deeper sense of inner peace and healing.

1. Recall the times in your life when you have been most deeply and unconditionally loved, accepted, or forgiven by certain people, and see those moments as intimations and incarnations of God's love, acceptance, or forgiveness. We don't come to know God's love, acceptance, and forgiveness solely by ourselves or only through the practice of prayer, but perhaps most poignantly through the "images of God" who have shown us special compassion, understanding, and magnanimity. These people might be one or both of your parents, a teacher, or a school guidance counselor from long ago. Or they could include a therapist, pastor, rabbi, spiritual director, friend, spouse, partner, or child.

Take a few minutes to call to heart and mind some of these people and the times when you were the recipient of their generous love, unconditional acceptance, or forgiveness. You might choose to remember with a pen and journal in hand. And as you remember, consider the fact that our God, who works through the created order and especially through people, was (is) loving, accepting, and forgiving you through them.

Pause, Ponder, or Practice

Take some time, right now if you can, to recall those special people whose love and concern for you was so very timely. Perhaps their support and compassion were especially meaningful to you during a time of illness or when a relationship came to an end or when you were facing a difficult situation at home or work. Or maybe it is those persons in whose presence you feel safe sharing some of your weaknesses and shortcomings because you know that they are supportive and understanding of you. Keep these memories in mind when you begin to question or doubt that God loves, accepts, and forgives you.

2. Trusting that the spirit of God is within you, speak to yourself, on behalf of God, words of love, acceptance, and forgiveness. Sometimes we have the mistaken impression that the biblical prophets and poets heard God speak to them in a way that God no longer speaks to us. But these God-impassioned, spirit-inspired individuals often used a literary device called an oracle in which they were utterly convinced that the words they spoke were the words God desired to speak through them.[2] A biblical oracle would frequently begin with "Thus says the Lord," and be followed by what the person was totally convinced God would say. Here's an example from the book of Isaiah: "Thus says the Lord: In a time of favor I have answered you, on a day of salvation I have helped you . . ." (Isa. 49:8a).

Because we have God's spirit within us, we, too, can allow God's voice to speak through us and to us. One simple way to do this is to allow God, through our own voice, to affirm us as in the following examples:

- I love you, (your name), unconditionally.
- I accept you, (your name), as you are.
- I forgive you, (your name), even before you ask me.
- I accept you, (your name), even though you continue to struggle with (name the struggle).

Initially, we might feel a little awkward or uncomfortable speaking to ourselves on behalf of God, because it's probably something most of us have never done before. But you and I just might experience a greater sense of divine love, acceptance, and forgiveness—as well as peace—if we are willing to give it a try. (Bridget Mary Meehan and Regina Madonna Oliver have written a short and beautiful book titled *Affirmations from the Heart of God* that is filled with an abundance of such affirmations. I recommend it very highly.[3])

3. Argue with God, wrestle with God, fight with God over whether or not you are inherently lovable, acceptable, and forgivable. In an earlier chapter we dialogued and argued with our inner critical voice. Now we play the role of a zealous and heartless prosecuting attorney and build our case before God as to why we are undeserving of divine love, acceptance, and forgiveness. For example, I would point out how often I have stumbled over the same destructive behavior patterns and how I sometimes don't even try to overcome these obstacles. "Take that, God! That ought to show you how unworthy I am of being loved. If I was making some progress, maybe you could still love me, but I'm not. In fact, I'm regressing. Therefore, I do not deserve any more love and forgiveness—at least not until I start to make some progress."

After vehemently arguing our unworthiness, we need to allow the inner voice of love, of God's spirit, to speak through us as a defense attorney, wise old judge, or passionate mother would, and allow God to tell us why we are lovable, acceptable, and forgivable. God might begin to respond to my argument by saying something to the effect: "Though you may want me to keep a scorecard of your sins and failings, it is not within my nature. You are more than hard enough on yourself, which, incidentally, makes it harder for you to believe that I can—and do— love and accept you as you are."

Like Jacob, who wrestled with a theophany (a manifestation or appearance of God) throughout an exhausting night, we, too, can wrestle with God through our dark nights when we question our lovability, forgivability, and acceptability. We can even get a little nasty and sarcastic as we fight, for we do not always have to be "nice" when encountering the divine. Perhaps at some point in the fight, which may occur on and off over the course of months or years or decades, we will receive a blessing and be able to hear and believe and accept the awesome news that God loves and accepts and forgives us *as we are!*

4. We can grow in our ability to accept God's love, acceptance, and forgiveness by reading from books that are spiritually, psychologically, and theologically sound. Books about God and prayer abound in this day and age. But not every book reflects the love of God, the God of the Bible. Our God, as Keith Magnuson, a pastor and friend of mine, periodically reminds his congregation, is *big*.

Similar to some of the religious leaders during Jesus' time, some contemporary authors who possess strong religious beliefs are prone to shrinking and limiting God's love to human size (or even smaller!). They sometimes succumb to moral legalism and biblical literalism by reducing the complexity of human existence to a simplistic and merciless code of right and wrong, saved and unsaved. Though usually well intentioned, the books they write are sometimes rigid, black-and-white, and fear-based and, as a result, may be more harmful than healing to those of us who are hungering for the God who is big.

The good news is that there is an abundance of good spiritual books available today that can help us grow in our ability to accept God's love, acceptance, and forgiveness. In the notes at the end of this book are some resources that I have found to be helpful and healing. I would like to share a brief excerpt from one of these books, a book that is geared toward women (although I have found it to be helpful as well): *Loving Yourself More: 101 Meditations for Women*. Here's a portion of the author's thirteenth reflection, which ties into what we have been discussing in this chapter: our desire to know God's love, acceptance, and forgiveness more deeply.

> No part of us, no feeling, is unlovable to God. So we can look at all the parts of ourselves and lovingly receive each. What part of yourself do you find hardest to

love? See or hear God loving that part of you"[4] (emphasis added).

Pause, Ponder, or Practice

What spiritual books and devotional materials have been most helpful to you during your life's journey? If you are reading and discussing this book with others, select a couple excerpts from one of your favorite books to share with members of your group. It could very well be that the words you have found to be so meaningful will touch someone in your group just as deeply.

5. Create a statement of divine love, acceptance, and forgiveness and read it aloud daily, periodically, or on an as needed basis. Earlier in the chapter we touched upon a suggested communal statement of our first identity as children of God, so that we might regain our theological balance when sin is overemphasized in our communities. This suggestion invites us to write a private statement of divine love, acceptance, and forgiveness, which we can change as our unique struggles and circumstances in life change. Here's the beginning of one that might help you to get started in writing your own.

Today, I accept the amazing grace that I am loved, accepted, and forgiven by God just as I am. I am accepted even though I am struggling with _____ and feel sad about it.

God is with me in the midst of my imperfections, my weaknesses, and shortcomings including _____, and at this moment is loving me into wholeness.

> God has completely forgiven me for the times I
> have hurt myself and others, including when I
> _____, and I fully accept God's forgiveness.

Perhaps during our quiet time or devotional time, we might regularly or periodically revise and meditatively read our self-created statement. It will be especially helpful to read it—and read it aloud so that we hear the words—during those times when we are down on ourselves or when we have suffered a setback and are struggling to feel God's love, acceptance, and forgiveness.

In these last three chapters we have addressed some of the issues involved in accepting and forgiving ourselves and others, as well as some of the obstacles that make it difficult to accept God's love, acceptance, and forgiveness. We have also identified a few ways that we might grow in our capacity to accept and forgive ourselves and others, and to accept the mind-boggling and heart-healing truth that we are unconditionally loved, accepted, and forgiven by our radically gracious God. In the next and last chapter, we will consider the vital role that prayer and meditation play in our quest for serenity.

Praying the Chapter

Merciful and compassionate God,
you'd think that I would jump at the chance
to accept your love, acceptance, and forgiveness,
but, as you know, I often turn away.
It's not because I don't want what you desire for me
or because I don't need this trio of life-giving gifts.
It's just that I feel so unworthy at times, so unlovable,

so unacceptable, so unforgivable.
Since you, God, are totally "other," I wonder if you
really know how hard it is to be a human being
with more than my share of weaknesses, shortcomings,
and bad habits that trip me up time and again.
Do you know what it is like to wrestle with some of them
for years—even decades—and not make a whole lot of progress
no matter how hard I try and how desperately I pray?
And when it comes to other people, most of them do not
love, accept, and forgive me as I am, so is it any wonder that
I periodically question your love, acceptance, and forgiveness?
Yet you keep inviting me to make the jump, to turn toward you
rather than away, so here I am asking for your help this day.

Help me to remember those special people in my life who have been
so extraordinarily loving, accepting, and forgiving of me.
Grace me with the inner vision to see that they are incarnations
and intimations of your greater love and to believe that you are loving
me through these remarkably gracious people.

Help me, too, to realize that I don't have to be an ideal
or perfect person in order to be loved by you,
but simply real, simply human, and a bit like Zacchaeus.
May I jump into your love as eagerly and
unself-consciously as he did,
but be patient with me for I am quite self-conscious and hesitant.

When I am feeling most unlovable, unacceptable, and unforgivable,
give me a fighting spirit to argue my unworthiness before you.
I trust that you can take my verbal jabs.
But as we fight, soften my heart softly,
so that I might come to believe more deeply
what is really quite unbelievable:
You love and accept and forgive me as I am!

Finally, give me the courage to say aloud to myself the words
that your spirit is whispering to me in my heart:
"I love you as you are."
"I accept you without any conditions whatsoever."
"I totally forgive you for the times you have hurt yourself and others."
Thank you, God, for being totally "other," for being like
the most tender and passionate of mothers.
Amen

For Reflection, Journaling, or Discussion

1. When is it most difficult for you to feel loved, accepted, and forgiven by God? What insights from this chapter might make it less difficult for you? When is it easiest for you to feel loved, accepted, and forgiven?

2. What Bible passages speak most powerfully to you of God's love? Spend some time reading, pondering, and praying over these passages, especially when you are most in need of divine love.

3. In whose lives have your words and actions been a reflection of God's love for them? At this moment who is in need of the love of God that flows through you? How might you be a channel of God's love this day?

CHAPTER 7

FINDING SERENITY THROUGH PRAYER AND MEDITATION

Prayer ... centers us in God and at the same time in ourselves.

—Roberta Bondi

AT ANY MOMENT WE SO CHOOSE, WE always have the option of turning to the spirit of God within us, to the one who is totally present to us and in whose presence we "live and move and have our being" (Acts 17:28). Because we reside within God's spirit and God's spirit resides within us, we are, quite literally, surrounded by and infused with the divine—though we may frequently fail to recognize God's presence. And this surrounding, infusing spirit of God is fully and irreversibly committed to the well being of creation and to its ongoing transformation. Furthermore, the divine spirit is intimately and actively involved in your life, in my life, and in every life.

Yet many of us struggle to believe the good news of both God's nearness and God's intimate, "spirited" involvement in our lives. It sometimes seems like God is really more "out there" somewhere rather than right here. It often appears that God is dispassionately observing life from afar, especially in times of heightened personal and communal suffering, rather than working passionately with us and within us to transform pain, sorrow, and heartache.

On more than one occasion, I have wondered how the Creator of the universe could be specifically involved in the details of my life when there are billions of other people in the world. And when I consider how little my problems usually are (though they seldom seem little to me!) in comparison to what many of my sisters and brothers experience, I start to entertain the discouraging thought that God may be busily attending to matters of much greater importance elsewhere. Maybe it's not realistic to hope for God's intimate involvement in our lives, in our personal problems, in our quests for inner and interpersonal peace, when the world is plagued by such huge problems as war, the AIDS crisis, poverty, oppression, homelessness, and the rapidly accelerating destruction of the environment.

But while it is quite normal to wrestle with periodic doubts such as these, we need to affirm and cling to the truth that God's omnipresent spirit is intimately with and within each of us. Our God is big enough to care for world peace and all of the world's bigger problems—though our efforts are absolutely critical—and small enough, intimate enough, to care for you and me and our yearnings for inner and interpersonal peace.

This understanding of God as spirit, as intimate, as with us and within us, and in whose omnipresence all of life is authored and nurtured, is central to our relationship with the divine and key to our understanding and practice of prayer and meditation. It is central to our relationship because we are relating to an omnipresent spirit-God that is always personally and intimately involved in our lives rather than to a "person-like" God who, like us, has limited energy and must make choices as to what will be given attention.[1] It is key to our understanding and practice of prayer and meditation because it means that we are neither launching our prayers to a distant God who is "out there" somewhere nor meditating in a spiritual vacuum, but communing with the indwelling, passionate, and all-encompassing spirit of the divine. And this spirit is eager to help us in every aspect of our lives including our quests for inner and interpersonal peace.

In the rest of this chapter, we will consider a few thoughts about prayer and meditation that can help set the theological stage for experiencing the omnipresence of God more fully. Then we will look at a few specific ways to pray and meditate so that we might come to know a deeper and more abiding sense of spirit-fed inner and interpersonal peace.

A Few Thoughts about Prayer

Both prayer and meditation have the potential to lead us to a peace-filled, healing silence and can help us experience a "daily-life-transforming" communion with the divine. Prayer and meditation often overlap and flow into each other; where one begins and the other ends is not always clear, in fact, such a distinction may only be in the "eye of the beholder"—or of the practitioner. Though they hold much in common, it may be helpful to say a few words about each of these spiritual practices. Here are four thoughts about prayer for your consideration.

We pray, in part, to strengthen our relationship with the divine. In an attempt to safeguard our limited understanding of the Ultimate Mystery, we often spend an inordinate amount of time formulating and defending our particular religious and spiritual beliefs. In fact, at times we can reach a point in which we become so intent upon defending our understanding of God against real or phantom opponents that we forget what the journey is all about: *relationship*.

God is not calling us to "correct" belief but is inviting each and every one of us to a reciprocal, empowering, living relationship with the divine. This is not to say that our specific beliefs and theological understandings are irrelevant; to the contrary, they are very important for most of us, myself included. But it is our *relationship* with God that is of ultimate importance and not our particular beliefs. One of the main reasons we pray is to strengthen this all-important relationship with our God, and to do that we need to spend some regular time communing with the divine.

Pause, Ponder, or Practice

Do you think that we sometimes spend too much time defining and defending our particular spiritual and religious beliefs to the detriment of our relationship with God and each other? Explain. How do your beliefs enhance your relationship with the divine and with others? How might they hinder your relationship with the divine and with others?

We pray in order to open up to and tap into God's love and power.[2] In the introduction, we spoke of those "naturally" centered folk in our midst who perhaps have access to a "mysterious private well of peace" from which they can draw serenity during life's stressful moments (see page 12). But the truth is we all have access to such an inner well, to the indwelling, in-welling, spirit of God, who is eager to help us know personal and interpersonal peace. Of course, knowing that we have the "spirit of God-well" within us is one thing, choosing to turn to and draw from this "well of peace" is quite another. Prayer can help us open up to and tap into this well from which we can draw divine love and strength to help us walk along the paths of—and to—peace.

Prayer changes as we change. Theologian Flora Slosson Wuellner writes, "We need not be troubled if the form and expression [of prayer] change. That is as it should be. . . . Because this is a living relationship with God and not a set of rules, your forms and methods of communication with God will change, evolve, expand, and flow in new ways."[3]

When an "old" way of praying is no longer helping us experience the peace and presence and power of God, we can learn a "new" way. The old way of praying is not wrong; we have simply outgrown it just like we have grown out of an old pair of jeans we used to wear in high school. We can learn some "new" ways to revitalize our relationship with the divine from a number of good books about prayer that are available to us or from our sisters and brothers—perhaps a spiritual director, pastor, rabbi, or friend—who might be able to help us.

Prayer cries out for an element of silence. I believe that there is a hole of varying sizes in each of our prayer lives that only silence can fill. While some have learned how to fill this hole, many of us have not. We easily talk to and with God, which is an important part of prayer, but many of us haven't learned how to be silent in the presence of God. In fact, we may not even know how to begin, so the "silence hole" in our prayer life goes unfilled and our prayer relationship remains, at least partially, unfulfilling as a result.

I have become convinced that my continued healing—we are all wounded and in need of healing—will come in large part by resting silently in God's tender embrace. I am equally convinced that my growth along the paths of inner and interpersonal peace will also require that I devote more of my prayer time to being silent before God. This may be true of you as well.

Perhaps nowhere else do prayer and meditation overlap and blend together as much as they do than when it comes to the healing realm of silence, so let us now turn our attention to a few thoughts about the latter.

A Few Thoughts about Meditation

Many of us hunger for and are intrigued by meditation, but we may not be exactly sure what it is. Perhaps like me, you have heard that prayer is talking to God and meditation is listening to God. But a number of prayer teachers stress that prayer primarily—or at least significantly—involves listening to God. So where does that leave meditation?

It's important to note right from the beginning that there is no universal definition of meditation. Just as definitions and descriptions for prayer abound, they do for meditation as well. Some people who speak or write about meditation seem to use the term interchangeably with contemplation, and emphasize being silent in God's presence. Others describe meditation as the process of mentally reflecting upon a particular scripture passage. And still others have different, and sometimes multiple, emphases. However, author, speaker, and spiritual guide J. P. Vaswani reassures us that "meditation is a most personal experience. . . . Every person meditates in his or her own way."[4]

I consider myself to be in the infant stages of meditation. And like a fussy infant, I often cry out for the "milk of meditation," yet in my lack of commitment to the practice of meditating, I sometimes resist the calming, nourishing, and satiating "bottle" that is always available to me. Even though I am inconsistent in my practice, I have tasted some of the benefits of this spiritual treasure and would like to share four thoughts that may be helpful to you as you begin or continue your practice.

Meditation involves resting quietly in the presence of God. Although we are always in the presence of God and never have to put ourselves in that presence, we are often unaware of the divine presence and are anything but restful—or peaceful. Even when we pray, we are often so mentally distracted and restless that we sometimes come away more discouraged with ourselves than refreshed and empowered by the spirit of God. But as we practice meditating, we will come to know the peaceful rest that is God's gift to us.

When it comes to meditation (and perhaps to prayer as well), we sometimes want to be instantly "successful" and free of any and all struggle. In a previous chapter we stressed that much of life, including our attempts to make progress with a persistent personal problem or painful emotion, involves a process. Yet when it comes to meditation, we usually experience countless distractions in our initial attempts and then quickly give up. But Vaswani says, "It is a difficult task to still the noise that is within: the clamor of conflicting thoughts."[5] If, however, we expect to encounter difficulties in our attempts to learn how to meditate, we are much less likely to become overly discouraged and quit before we reap the rewards of perseverance.

Pause, Ponder, or Practice

Have you ever, like me, tried to meditate or experience silent prayer only to quickly give up because your thoughts bounced around out of control? If so, describe your experience. Does it make sense that we will encounter difficulties in prayer and meditation just like we do in most other worthwhile endeavors? Why or why not?

The art of meditation requires that we practice on some kind of consistent basis. As with any art form, we need to practice meditating on a regular basis if we expect to make progress. Whether this is daily, twice a day, or two or three times a week, devoting some consistent time to meditation can help us grow in inner peace.

Many meditation teachers, including Vaswani, suggest meditating for fifteen minutes initially and then increasing it to a half hour or hour daily. While I respect the fact that these teachers have had much more experience with meditation than I have, I think that five or ten minutes is a more reasonable starting point for many of us. I have also found that spending ten or fifteen minutes two or three times a week can be very refreshing.

We need to be gentle with ourselves as we experience distractions. Most of us have very active minds, and our thoughts, at times, seem to lie beyond the realm of our control. The practice of meditation will enable us to gradually harness, quiet, and steer our thoughts in positive directions so that we might know both the wonders of interior silence and the peace of God. But as we practice, especially in the beginning, our thoughts are likely to become even more wild and out of control.

As always, God sets before us the choice of life or death. Getting down on ourselves, scolding ourselves, and giving up is a choice for death that will kill the seeds of meditation before they have had a chance to grow. Being gentle with ourselves, encouraging ourselves, and continuing to practice is a choice for life that will nurture these same seeds and elicit abundant growth.

Wuellner suggests that some of our distractions may point to something in our lives that is in need of healing, which we can consciously bring before God. "If they seem [to be] trivial distractions, don't use force. Smile at them as you would at a little child or an animal at play, and return to the Center while they play at the edges of your consciousness."[6] And Vaswani offers these encouraging words: "If for a whole hour I have done no more than bring the mind back to the Lord every time it has moved afar, I have not spent the hour in vain."[7]

Finding Serenity through Prayer and Meditation

Prayer and meditation, rather than being a substitute for prudent—and sometimes passionate—action, can inspire and strengthen us to take the sometimes quite difficult steps we need to take in order to strengthen or restore our inner and interpersonal peace. For example, through the grace and power of God that we are able to tap into through these interdependent disciplines, we can summon the necessary courage to confront someone about his or her hurtful behavior. Or we can receive the grace to reclaim the humility we need in order to make amends to someone we have hurt. We are also able to rest in God's love and experience a sense of peace-filled renewal when we turn to prayer and meditation. What follows are four suggested practices to help us tap into the indwelling, peace-nurturing spirit of God.

In order to regain or strengthen your sense of serenity, prayerfully and meditatively repeat and affirm one or all of the following four prayer phrases: "God is with me," "God is within me," "I am in God," and "God loves me as I am." Close your eyes and slowly repeat one or more of these phrases over and over. You might do so in conjunction with your breathing or by allowing for a pregnant pause after each repetition, so that the words and the love and presence of God they point to become more deeply rooted in your heart. Say and pray the words aloud if you like. Meditate upon the potential implications that these simple truths can have in your life each day. How might you live your life differently this day or what creative risks might you be called to take because you know at the deepest level of your being that God is with you? How might you be better able to love yourself and others as you and they are because you have meditated upon God's unwavering love for you as you are?

At first glance, these prayer phrases may appear to be self-centered and selfish, but they aren't. They help us become rooted in the presence and power of God's love, so that we can be bearers of that presence and love in all of our daily encounters and interactions. They center us in God and, like a stone that has a rippling effect when it is thrown into a lake, these "self-focused" prayer phrases can empower us to have a loving, rippling effect in the lives of others. And, of course, we can always substitute the personal pronoun in each of these phrases with the name of someone else, whether it be a loved one or an enemy, and pray and meditate in an intercessory manner whenever we are so moved.

Prayerfully and meditatively repeat and affirm other short phrases to help you deal with, defend against, or

recover from specific stressful, upsetting, or anxious moments. The beauty of these short phrases is that they are short enough to commit to memory, practical enough to use during difficult times, and meaning-filled enough to help us tap into the richness of the spirit of God within. For example, in times of transition we might prayerfully repeat and meditate upon a phrase such as "God is guiding me." When fear is overwhelming us, we might pray, "God's spirit fills me with courage." In times of desolation we might pray and meditate upon such soothing words as "God's love comforts me," and experience the unfathomable tenderness of God in the process. And to remind us of the fact that God desires that we be one with all people and to help us grow in this oneness each day, especially with those we have deemed enemy or "other," we might contemplate the words, "We are all one."

Use a prayer word or phrase to help you experience silent prayer or meditation. Because our minds are almost always generating thoughts, a single word or short prayer phrase can provide a focus point for the word-dependent part of our minds to cling to. Some possible words and phrases that can help us become anchored in the silent presence of God include: "Jesus," "Lord Jesus," "Christ, our light," "Christ-Sophia," "Come, Holy Spirit," "God is love," "God is with me," "Maranatha" (Aramaic for "Our Lord, come"), "The Lord is my shepherd," "God is light," "Abba" (Aramaic for "Father"), "Imma" (Aramaic for "Mother"), "Adonai" (Hebrew for "Lord"), and "Peace, be still."

We can use such a word or phrase to assist us in becoming more quiet within and to help us rest silently in the refreshing presence of God. We can set the word aside when we have become more quiet, and we can pick the word up again when our minds begin to drift away and become more restless. We can also call upon the word throughout the day, rather than limiting its usage to our focused period of prayer or meditation.

Many prayer teachers recommend using the same word or phrase each day rather than changing from one to another. You may have to experiment a little bit in order to find the one that speaks to you and that leads you to a point in your encounters with the divine in which you don't need to speak. I usually rely upon the phrase "God is with me" or "God is with us." However, I am not hesitant to use a different word or phrase on any given day if it would be better for me to do so. For example, when I am feeling unworthy of love, I will use the phrase "God loves me" as my anchor and pathway to inner silence.

Pause, Ponder, or Practice

What prayer word or prayer phrase might serve as your anchor and pathway to resting silently in the presence of God? Take a few minutes right now if you can and allow this word or phrase to help you experience a taste of interior silence and the love of God that is beyond all words.

Envision the light of God or the light of Christ shining on you, enfolding you, or arising within you as you pray and meditate. You might choose to light a candle to symbolize this light. Or you could imagine yourself sitting in a chair at sunrise facing an eastern window as the sun rises. The sun would represent the light of God's love for you as it slowly rises and envelops you in its warmth. (This can be done even on the rainiest and dreariest of days.) Or you might envision the divine light surrounding, descending upon, or arising within you in some other manner.

You might also choose to use a verse from the Bible, such as "The Lord is my light and my salvation" (Ps. 27:1) or "The light shines in the darkness" (John 1:5) to help you enter and experience this loving light more fully. Or you might generate your own light-enhancing prayer statement, such as "The healing light of God envelops my entire being."

Envisioning the light of God or Christ is not only healing for ourselves, but it can also be a wonderful way to pray for the healing, well being, and inner peace of others. Sometimes we don't know what to say or pray when someone is facing a terminal illness or when someone has lost a loved one to tragedy or even when someone is not suffering but may still be on our heart and mind. We sometimes search for words in our time of prayer when we don't need to say anything. We can simply envision the divine light enfolding the person for whom we are praying. And we can envision our light joining God's light in upholding this person in love—and in peace.

A Final Note

Prayer and meditation are indispensable tools for our individual and collective journeys to inner and interpersonal peace. They can help us tap into and draw from an infinitely greater and deeper source of peace than our own—God's. And I believe that we can—and will!—know a greater measure of serenity and find ourselves better equipped to face life's challenges, stresses, and inevitable broken moments as we turn to this caring, omnipresent, indwelling spirit of God. For this amazing God of ours is ever eager to flood our very being to the point of overflowing with "the peace of God, which surpasses all understanding" (Phil. 4:7).

Praying the Chapter

Omnipresent and intimate Spirit-God,
I often find it difficult to believe that your spirit
permeates all of creation and even resides within me.
For most of my life, I've suspected that you are
really more "out there" somewhere rather than
right here with me, with us, in the thick of life.

Teach me to look inward as well as outward
for signs of your caring and empowering presence.
When suffering—my own as well as the world's—leads me
to question your involvement, help me to remember
that you are wholeheartedly and irreversibly committed to the
well being of your entire creation, of which I am a part.

Loving God, may I believe in the depths of my heart that
whenever and however I pray, I am strengthening
my relationship with you as I open up to
your daily-life-transforming love.
When my old prayer ways fail to fit me any longer,
lead me to new prayer paths so that I might
tap into your peace and presence and power.
Help me, too, to listen to the cries for silence
in my prayer life and to begin filling these prayer
holes by risking wordless encounters with you.

Teach me how to meditate in my own unique way. I've often
hungered for meditation but have quickly grown discouraged
and given up when my thoughts have refused to settle down.
I have wanted instant success, which I now realize is rather silly.
I ask that you reveal to me a prayer word or prayer phrase that
can help me rest silently in your tender embrace.

Thank you for your healing light that surrounds and upholds
all of creation, including my sisters and brothers
who are suffering at this very moment. Help me to envision
this light in my life, especially when I am yearning
for a sense of your presence
but words only seem to get in the way.

Finally, I pray that you will continue to lead each and every one
of us along the paths to inner and interpersonal peace
and to peace throughout our world.
Fill our hearts to the point of overflowing with your
peace which, indeed, passes all understanding.
Amen

For Reflection, Journaling, or Discussion

1. This chapter stressed that God is intimately and passionately involved in the care and transformation of the world, including every life. When have you experienced God's nearness? When have you felt like God might be busy attending to matters of "greater" importance elsewhere?

2. Have you ever tried to envision the light of God or the light of Christ during your times in prayer and meditation? Do you think that envisioning this light can be a helpful way to pray for yourself and others, especially when words are not forthcoming? Why or why not?

3. How have prayer and meditation helped restore or strengthen your sense of inner peace? Do you have any insights about how prayer and meditation can help us find serenity? If you are reading and discussing this book in a group setting, be willing to share your wisdom with others.

Sources for Quotations

Page 17: from *Healing Wisdom: Insight & Inspiration for Anyone Facing Illness* by Greg Anderson. New York: Penguin Books, 1994.

Page 34: from *Positive Thoughts: Living Your Life to the Fullest* by Armand Eisen. Kansas City, Missouri: Andrews and McNeel, 1995.

Page 55: from *Healing Wisdom: Insight & Inspiration for Anyone Facing Illness* by Greg Anderson. New York: Penguin Books, 1994. (Original quote is "It's not that I am afraid of dying. I just don't want to be there when it happens.")

Page 78: from *Healing Wisdom: Insight & Inspiration for Anyone Facing Illness* by Greg Anderson. New York: Penguin Books, 1994.

Page 100: from *Healing Wisdom: Insight & Inspiration for Anyone Facing Illness* by Greg Anderson. New York: Penguin Books, 1994.

Page 141: from *To Love as God Loves: Conversations with the Early Church* by Roberta Bondi. Minneapolis: Fortress Press, 1987.

NOTES

Chapter 1

1. Douglas John Hall, *God & Human Suffering* (Minneapolis: Augsburg Publishing House, 1986), 53–55.

2. Kenneth S. Leong, *The Zen Teachings of Jesus* (New York: Crossroad, 1995), 14–15.

3. Melody Beattie, *The Language of Letting Go* (Center City, Minnesota: Hazelden, 1990), 155.

Chapter 2

1. An excellent book about the positive and negative shadow is David Richo's *Shadow Dance* (Boston: Shambhala Publications, 1999).

2. Louis Savary & Patricia Berne, *Prayer Medicine* (Barrytown, New York: Station Hill Press, 1980), 133.

3. Kathleen Wall & Gary Ferguson, *Lights of Passage* (New York: HarperCollins, 1994), 6.

4. John Powers, *Seeking Inner Peace: The Art of Facing Your Painful Emotions* (Mystic, Connecticut: Twenty-Third Publications, 1987), 4.

5. "What a Friend We Have in Jesus." Words: Joseph M. Scriven, ca. 1855; music: Charles C. Converse, 1868.

Chapter 3

1. Fran Ferder, *Words Made Flesh: Scripture, Psychology, and Human Communication* (Notre Dame: Ave Maria Press, 1986), 60.

2. Kenneth L. Bakken, *The Journey Into God: Healing and Christian Faith* (Minneapolis: Augsburg Fortress, 2000), 68.

3. David Richo, *How to Be an Adult: A Handbook on Psychological and Spiritual Integration* (Mahwah, New Jersey: Paulist Press, 1991), 37.

4. Richard J. Gilmartin, *Pursuing Wellness, Finding Spirituality* (Mystic, Connecticut: Twenty-Third Publications, 1996), 48–49.

5. If you or a friend or loved one are going through a difficult time, I highly recommend reading a couple of Henri Nouwen's brief reflections in *The Inner Voice of Love: A Journey Through Anguish to Freedom* (New York: Doubleday, 1996).

6. A concise and practical guide to the practice of visualization is Shakti Gawain's *Creative Visualization* (New York: Bantam Books, Inc., 1978).

Chapter 4

1. From *Wellsprings: A Book of Spiritual Exercises* by Anthony de Mello copyright © 1984 by Anthony de Mello, S.J. Used by permission of Doubleday, a division of Random House Inc.

2. Douglas Bloch, *Listening to Your Inner Voice* (Center City, Minnesota: Hazelden, 1991), 122.

3. John O'Donohue, *Anam Cara* (New York: HarperCollins, 1997), 13–14.

4. Bloch, 11–16.

5. de Mello, 53–55.

Chapter 5

1. Gary Egeberg, *From Self-Care to Prayer: 31 Refreshing Spiritual Tips* (Mystic, Connecticut: Twenty-Third Publications, 1999), 63.

2. Judy Logue, *Forgiving the People You Love to Hate* (Liguori, Missouri: Liguori Publications, 1997), 19–20.

3. Thich Nhat Hanh, *Living Buddha, Living Christ* (New York: Riverhead Books, 1995), 75–79.

4. Terry D. Cooper, *I'm Judgmental You're Judgmental: Healing Our Condemning Attitudes* (Mahwah, New Jersey: Paulist Press, 1999), 48.

5. Cooper, 15, 17.

Chapter 6

1. Roberta Bondi, *To Love as God Loves: Conversations with the Early Church* (Minneapolis: Fortress Press, 1987), 85–86.

2. This concept comes from Margaret Nutting Ralph's book, *Discovering Prophecy and Wisdom: The Books of Isaiah, Job, Proverbs, and Psalms* (Mahwah, New Jersey: Paulist Press, 1993).

3. Bridget Mary Meehan & Regina Madonna Oliver, *Affirmations from the Heart of God* (Liguori, Missouri: Liguori Publications, 1998).

4. Virginia Ann Froehle, *Loving Yourself More: 101 Meditations for Women* (Notre Dame: Ave Maria Press, 1993), 33–34.

Chapter 7

1. I am indebted to Marcus Borg for pointing out that when we use the word *person* to talk about God (e.g., three persons, one God), we sometimes envision God as *being* a person (e.g., father) as we unintentionally forget that we are using metaphorical language. By using the phrase *Spirit-God* or *Spirit of God*, we can retain our belief in God's *personal* father-like or mother-like, etcetera, care for us while strengthening our understanding of divine omnipresence, of the "Spirit that

blows where it will." This understanding can help us let go of the notion of a sometimes present, sometimes absent *person-like* God who may be too busy to attend to us, and embrace the understanding of the Spirit's immanent, caring omnipresence. See his fine book, *The God We Never Knew: Beyond Dogmatic Religion to a More Authentic Contemporary Faith* (San Francisco: HarperSanFrancisco, 1998).

2. Gary Egeberg, *The Pocket Guide to Prayer* (Minneapolis: Augsburg Fortress, 1999), 21.

3. Flora Slosson Wuellner, *Prayer, Stress, & Our Inner Wounds* (Nashville: The Upper Room, 1995), 19, 24.

4. J. P. Vaswani, *The Way of Abhyasa: Meditation in Practice* (Liguori, Missouri: Triumph Books, 1995), 31–32. The word *Abhyasa* is a Sanskrit word that means "practice," in this case learning how to meditate by practicing. This book is among the most concise, easy to read, encouraging, and practical guides to meditation that I have come across. No matter what your spiritual or religious affiliation may be, you are likely to find an abundance of insights and practical suggestions to help you meditate within the bounds of your tradition.

5. Vaswani, 17.

6. Wuellner, 24.

7. Vaswani, 20.

OTHER RESOURCES FROM AUGSBURG

The Pocket Guide to Prayer by Gary Egeberg
152 pages, 0-8066-3958-X

This book offers practical suggestions you can use right away to foster a more satisfying prayer life. A variety of tools are provided to help nurture and expand our unique ways of praying.

'Tis a Gift to Be Simple: Embracing the Freedom of Living with Less by David Sorensen and Barbara DeGrote-Sorensen
128 pages, 0-8066-2573-2

This book offers help for all of us who would like to make our lives less complicated but aren't sure how to begin.

Soul Gardening: Cultivating the Good Life by Terry Hershey
168 pages, 0-8066-4037-5

Open the gate to the garden of your soul. Terry Hershey's stories will lead you to nurture your soul and renew your sense of what it means to live "the good life."

Available wherever books are sold.
To order these books directly, contact:
1-800-328-4648 • www.augsburgfortress.org
Augsburg Fortress, Publishers
P.O. Box 1209, Minneapolis, MN 55440-1209